MORE THAN CASHFLOW:
The *Real* Risks and Rewards of Profitable
Real Estate Investing

ISBN 978-0-9919060-1-7

Printed and bound in Canada

MORE THAN CASHFLOW:

The *Real* Risks and Rewards of Profitable

Real Estate Investing

By Julie Broad

STICK HORSE PUBLISHING

2013

To my Grandpa Broad.
More than any property he ever owned or
any business he ever ran, nothing was more
important to him than his family.

PREFACE

I may be alone in admitting it, but I know I am not alone in feeling it: there are days when I think a job at Starbucks would be the way to go. The smell of freshly ground coffee all day long and minimal work stress to take home at the end of the day – sometimes the idea is appealing.

There are days when I am stressed, annoyed and exhausted with everything that's happening in our real estate investing business. And of course everything happens at once – from contractor issues to tenant troubles to renovation surprises. It never seems to get spread out in nice manageable intervals.

Don't misunderstand what I'm saying: leaving my "regular" job was the best decision I have ever made. It was also the single biggest leap of faith in myself that I have ever taken.

But here's the piece that I think a lot of people don't understand about leaps of faith....

Real estate didn't make that leap from worker bee to entrepreneur possible – I did. We hadn't reached that magic number of properties to ensure we were secure; nor did we have anywhere near the cash coming in monthly for me to comfortably say "no thanks" to my six figure salary.

I just reached a point in my career and in my life where, although I had put my heart and soul into my job; instead of feeling appreciated and rewarded, I felt scolded and controlled.

Our real estate portfolio was a good size, but it wasn't where it needed to be for the breadwinner of the house (me) to leave my large pay cheque behind. However, I don't know if I would ever have been able to leave my job if I had waited for our real estate business to be at a point where it could replace my day job income.

It simply doesn't work that way.

It wasn't until I left, and then convinced my husband Dave to leave his job too, that our real estate business really gained strength. *For us to become great real estate investors, it took our complete focus and dedication, and the tension that comes with knowing "we have to make it work because there's no back-up plan."*

Why start the book with that introduction?

I want you to know that "real estate" is probably not the answer to the question you are asking. Being a full time real estate investor is not a destination – it's a vehicle to get you somewhere.

I've only just begun to realize this as I ask myself "What next?" Because the thing is – 10 years ago the life I am living right now WAS my destination.

I start with this thought because: first, it highlights the fact that this book is going to be different than any other real estate book you've ever read; and second, I used to do a lot of things so people would like me (and not just little things like going out for pub food when I really wanted Thai food). I am talking about buying properties and cars and being involved in businesses that weren't what I wanted – for the simple reason that I wanted to be *liked* by certain people.

I also used to write articles that I knew people wanted to read.

In other words, I would make certain practices okay just because everyone did them. I didn't want to ruffle feathers or have someone be unhappy with me.

This book, however, is not written so you will like me or be happy with me. I've decided it's more important to be boldly honest than it is to worry about what you or anybody else that reads this will think.

Even though there's a risk of upsetting everyone, from my coaching clients to our investors to friends in the industry, I feel I have to write this book. I want you to know some critical details about real estate investing either before you get into it or before you get in too deep. My only objective is to help you make better, more informed decisions around your real estate investing choices.

I am not promising you secrets that will make you rich, and I am not guaranteeing that this book will make you a successful real estate investor. However, I believe that, armed with an honest account of what it's like to be a real estate investor, you will make better decisions. It's very hard to choose the best decisions and solutions when the information available isn't 100% open and honest.

ACKNOWLEDGEMENTS

When I sat down to write the book, I had no idea that was going to be the easiest part of the whole process! I had no idea what I was getting into. I am still in shock at the monumental amount of effort, support and creativity it takes to turn words into a book worth reading. I owe this accomplishment to many people who have supported me and helped me get it over the finish line.

I absolutely must start with a huge hug of gratitude to Dave Peniuk, an incredible husband, dedicated business partner, and my number one supporter. This book is his too. Maybe he didn't sit down and write the book but he had to put up with me while I did – and that was probably even more difficult than writing. More significantly, he's lived through the experiences, lessons and achievements right there with me. The stories in this book are as much his as they are mine.

Hugs and thanks to those who directly helped me with this book: Jemima Codrington, Dee Allamong, Iryna Spica, Cathy Reed, Ruth-Anne Broad, Krish Centeno, Zander Robertson and to the designers at CrowdSpring. There was a lot of work involved with this book and you were a huge help!

Without Philip McKernan I would have written the wrong book. I was so close to writing what would have been easy to market not what needed to be said. This book is exactly what I think real estate investors need to read and it's something I'm enormously proud of. Thank you to him for his friendship, guidance and never settling for anything less than what's real.

Also, a big shout out to the brilliance of master influencer and persuader Kevin Hogan for saving me from some big blunders on this book. So thrilled to have you in my corner – thank you!

Massive thanks to many other amazing people who have played a part in helping me directly and indirectly create this book: Greg Habstritt, Deb Cole, Mark Ford, Mary Ellen Tribby, and Linda Andres. Finally, I have to thank some of my amazing VIP coaching clients. You have given ME so much support and encouragement throughout this process – I'm hugely grateful to work with smart, giving and energetic people like you Matthew Tynan, Tim Collins, Jeff White, Christina Kadin, Ian Kennedy, Diana Cortes, Ryan Gaucher, Wes Greenwood, Carmen Webb, Cheryl MacCalder, Lori McKee, Michelle Pink, Jeff Trapp and so many others. Thank you.

TABLE OF CONTENTS

Preface   vii

Introduction   1

1   In the Hotel Room Where It All Began   9
2   The Biggest Myths In Real Estate   17
3   How to Become a Full-Time Real Estate Investor –
     Even Though You Might Not Actually
     Want to Be One   35
4   Where to Invest   59
5   How to Create Deals That Make Money   79
6   Analyzing Real Estate Deals   113
7   Increasing Cash Flow With Rent to Own   129
8   Property Red Flags   137
9   Let's Make a Deal   149
10   Getting the Money   171
11   Tenants, Toilets, and Tons of Fun With
     Property Managers   201
12   Managing Your Property or Your
     Property Manager   221
13   Systems For Success   233
14   Where are the Ladies?   243
15   Is Real Estate For You?   255

     Recommended Resources   263
     About the Author   268

INTRODUCTION

MY STORY OF MANSLAUGHTER AND A CRACK HOUSE

By the time we read Dave's name in the paper under the headline of *Absentee Landlord Pleads Guilty in Fire Code Violations*, it was almost funny. We weren't laughing though; especially when the article went on to describe our property as a crack house.

What happened to us began several years before that moment. Dave had watched a late night infomercial promoting a free real estate investing seminar at a nearby hotel room and signed us up.

A famous author's company was coming into town to teach potential investors how to do deals with no money down and without the banks. At the time, we'd already invested all the money we had into our first two properties and I was in school. We didn't have money or the ability to qualify for much of a mortgage so their offer was appealing.

That seminar was the beginning of a decade-long journey during which we tried to figure out what the heck we were doing wrong – i.e., why was real estate investing such bloody hard work?

We didn't *really* believe it was as easy as the infomercial or that first seminar made it seem; but we also didn't think it was going to be as much work as it was. We figured we were missing something or doing something wrong.

After doing nearly $15,000,000 in real estate transactions in the last eleven years, and acquiring a new investment property every six weeks for the last three years, deals are easier; but they still take work. And the more properties you own (even though your team probably grows and gets better) the more work you have to do.

However, through sheer exhaustion and frustration, we finally uncovered one simple secret that makes real estate investing easier and easier – but make no mistake about it; it's still work.

In this book I will share every detail of that secret with you. I'll walk you step by step through some of our biggest lessons and lay out *exactly* how to prevent the same problems from arising in your investment life (later, it makes a great story to say you found yourself in court pleading guilty to fire code violations after your property manager turned your property into a crack house, but it is *not* fun to live through it). I am also going to tell you some important truths, ones seldom shared in the real estate industry.

I've recently accepted an ugly truth about the real estate education industry: *A lot of people – even good people – tell lies.* And many people with "celebrity status" basically *sell* their names, so you can't automatically trust what they say simply because you like their TV show or agree with the stated principles in their best-selling book.

Real estate investing is *not* easy. There are a lot of things you can do to make it *easier*, but there is no one trick or secret strategy that will enable you to make easy money. Real estate investment takes ongoing work and dedication.

I can't count the number of times I've heard this question: "How can I make some quick money with real estate?" I've also encountered too many folks who think that they need to buy 17 properties to be successful; or that believe that they "just" need to earn $10,000 per month of passive income from their real estate investments and then they'll be set for life.

Honestly, I don't blame these people for asking questions

like this or having this kind of mindset. There are a boatload of people out there who are busy making real estate investing sound easy. They exude happiness (as if their life was all roses), meanwhile they are stressing out about their vacant properties and worry ing about their bills. Some of these presenters stand on stage pretending they are experts, while behind the scenes they are dealing with money-losing properties and unhappy investors.

The good news for you is that the real estate world is changing. I notice the shift. I see a rise in the number of people entering the education industry that really care about YOU, the student and client. What's more, you're probably smarter than Dave and I were a decade ago, and your scam alert meter is probably better. And with social media, online searching, and blogging becoming so easy and so prevalent, I think it's getting more difficult to run a real estate education business scamming people out of their money, as has been so prevalent in the past ... but I still see it happening.

One of our VIP coaching clients laid out their portfolio for us in the summer of 2012. The shit they learned to do – and there is absolutely NO other word to describe what they were taught – was horrible. They had bought a significant number of properties and leveraged them for a sizeable amount more than each property was worth using second mortgages. The lenders for these high risk second mortgages were their friends and family. This practice is unethical and extremely risky. It's hard to believe anyone would do this, if you didn't already know what kind of things are sometimes taught in this industry (in this particular case, the investors were taught these tactics in 2011, not way back when). These investors trusted what they were taught in the course because it was associated with the name of a very famous person. For them, trusting the course was a costly mistake - financially and emotionally.

I started this book over a year ago but then lost interest. I started thinking that there were so many real estate books already and why did people need another book? But after we sat down with these two people and realized what they had just learned to do – and WHY they did it despite being very honest people of high integrity, I realized that *there definitely was a need for this book. I had a mission to fulfill.*

Not long after, we attended a real estate information session given by a Canadian investor and speaker – one of those guys who's famous because he's on TV and people automatically trust him becausee he's not an American guru. I tell the story later in the book, but I actually left that session in tears because *people were told lie after lie to get them to sign up for his course.* And while the course may not be all bad and may have some useful material, I knew *the buyers would not get the results they hoped for based on the crap promised at that information session.*

After seeing the potential harm that could come from that session, it took me no time at all to finish this book. Real estate is a great way to build your financial security. In fact, I'm convinced it's the best asset class in the world to own, especially Canadian real estate. But it's not a get-rich-quick tool, nor is it likely to be the solution you're looking for – to solve the problems you think it will solve.

When I first got into real estate, I was looking for a longer term solution to financial security. I was 24 and about to quit my job and go back to school to do my MBA. I wanted my money to work for me while I was in school. I believe I started out with the right plan; I called it FREEDOM 35. I wanted to build a strong enough portfolio so that by the age of 35 I would have choices, and I wouldn't have to work for someone else if I didn't want to. I was dating Dave at the time (we married in 2008) and I shared my plans with him. He had already bought an investment property with his Mom when he was 19; so the idea of real estate as an investment made perfect sense to him. So we dove into real estate investing together.

We started on a good path, but got distracted by the promises and lies. We began to believe real estate would make us rich – and fast. We chased deals. We sought out motivated sellers. We tried to make fast cash using the assignment strategy (now most people call this wholesaling). These tactics worked for a while, but overall we created more problems than wealth, security, or freedom. Then we had to dig in and clean up the messes we'd made.

Now we enjoy a lot of comforts in life – but we are not filthy rich by any stretch of the imagination. We still have months where we're juggling the cash outflow with the cash inflow because that is just how it is – a bigger portfolio means more money flowing in, but it also means more money is flowing out when things need repaired or problems need solved.

For the most part, we now live a life we love. We control our time, have a great relationship, and have friends and family we cherish. But make no mistake – we still have our share of totally crappy days. We still get concerned about how we'll pay for a massive problem or a big renovation project. And, we still get irritated by tenants who say one thing and do another.

But we know how to create money and we know we can tackle big problems. We also don't experience half as many irritations as we did when we were in jobs that we didn't love, controlled by people that we didn't want to work for anymore. The power and confidence that this gives us is enormously empowering and freeing. We know we're up for any challenge and we're always excited about what might be coming up next.

That's my wish for you too. And the cool part is: if you are willing to hit a few bumps along the way, I can direct you to a straightforward path to finding good deals, funding those deals, and having awesome tenants.

MY PROMISE AND MY DISCLOSURE

In this book I promise to tell you the truth. So before we go any further, let me make a full and clear disclosure. My husband and I run a real estate education business (revnyou.com) AND we invest in residential real estate, primarily in Nanaimo, B.C., Canada. We've been investing together since the fall of 2001 and have been living off of our real estate investments since 2008. As of 2011, our education business is also beginning to contribute positively to our financial situation.

We are very selective about whom we work with in both businesses – we turn away as many people as we work with – but we are always happy to open our doors to a new coaching client who has goals that are in alignment with what we can do to help them. And we actively seek joint venture partners and private investors with capital to invest in our real estate deals.

Of course I have certain personal biases, but with regard to basic real estate practices, I am working hard to write this in a way that is straightforward and unbiased. *I want to give it to you straight because not enough people do.* I want to tell you *the whole story* and not just part of the story.

I'm going to share:

- Some thoughts I have about your J-O-B;
- Why real estate investing might be the worst thing you can do;
- Why Passive Income is total B.S.;
- What every new investor needs to know before signing up for any investing course;
- The simple success secret no get-rich-quick guru ever teaches;
- Why "no money down" doesn't mean it won't cost you – and what to do about it;
- Three proven strategies you need to know to build your wealth through real estate (become an area expert, create a great team, keep it simple);
- The good, the bad and the sometimes ugly side of real estate investing as a couple – and how to enjoy more good than bad.

Plus, if I haven't scared you away from real estate totally, I will lay out a plan for you to use real estate to create more wealth, financial security and freedom – step by step. These are the same steps we teach our coaching clients. It's the exact plan many people just like you have used either to improve their existing portfolio or to get started.

In case you're just skimming this to figure out if you want to read on … I want you to know that if you stop reading here, you'll never find out why we considered calling this book "Murder, Lies & Eviction Notices" and you'll miss some entertaining *true* stories.

So keep reading – I won't make you rich overnight, but I will open your eyes and mind to some different ways of looking at real estate investing – and we will have fun together!

CHAPTER ONE

IN THE HOTEL ROOM
WHERE IT ALL BEGAN

D ave and I had just moved across the country from British
Columbia so I could pursue my MBA at York University in
Toronto, Ontario. It was early 2002. We had already purchased
the condo we were living in and an investment property, but
neither property was going to make us rich anytime soon.

Dave was dreaming of the day when he didn't have to work
for anyone. He despised working for "the man" and having to
jump when someone told him to jump.

What came next began when Dave was home one evening
watching TV while waiting for me to come home from school.
The infomercial playing in front of him promised instant cash,
super easy success, and freedom. It even used the magic
words: *you can do this without having to invest any money.* That was important to both of us because I had just quit my
job to go back to school and we'd sunk all our money into our
condo and the investment property.

We figured that if even half of what the get-rich-quick guru
promised was true, Dave could be kissing his 9-to-5 job good-
bye in twelve months or less. He eagerly attended the free seminar to learn how to do the no-money-down deals.

The free seminar didn't teach him anything, but he did hear

a lot of great stories about what his life would be like when he became rich. He heard stories about how people with less cash and assets than he had were able to turn the seminar into real estate gold practically overnight.

He quickly signed us up for the $2,000 weekend seminar and we were excited about going.

The weekend session taught just enough about a dozen different strategies for us to realize that we didn't know *anything*. Given that we were committed to our success as investors, it was clear that the only thing that made sense at this point was to sign ourselves up for the $20,000 mentorship program. With this program, we would learn all the details of the strategies we'd heard about and also have a mentor help us along the way. Besides, the teachers of the course assured us that our first deal would pay for the cost of the program, no problem.

By the way, even after spending $20,000 on these programs, we never did meet the big name celebrity behind the seminars. We never even saw him from a distance, and I don't think our mentor had ever met him either. On top of that, our supposed mentor didn't seem to be much of an investor himself. He claimed to have owned some apartment buildings, but he seemed to live out of a rental car. At the time, we believed some of the stories he told us about his investments, but when I look back now as an experienced investor, I think he was just following a script.

In that regard, I don't think what I call the "real estate guru industry" has changed at all. The big name U.S.-based courses still come to Canada and sell out, based solely on the "name" behind their program. Many of the mentors that you pay big bucks to work with are not experienced investors themselves. CBC Newswatch did a big report on this exact issue in 2010. Here's the link to the report: http://www.cbc.ca/news/story/2010/01/28/consumer-rich-dad-poor-dad-marketplace.html.

Right now, one of the saddest things in the real estate guru industry is that one of the most trusted names – the author whose book has put more people into real estate investing than any other – has absolutely nothing to do with the courses that have his name on them. The company that uses his business name for their courses licensed the name after they got into hot water over what they were teaching under a different guru's name.

We have many clients come to us, frustrated and discouraged, after trying to implement the strategies they learned from that course or another similar one. They have spent big bucks on a mentor who is trying to put them into deals that are high risk, hard to do, or just don't work in Canada. Worse, we know two people who put the teachings into practice and ended up overleveraged on their entire portfolio – in some cases as much as 136% over the value of the property! The most awful part for them is that they borrowed money from their friends and family – which is a not an uncommon scenario. They are paying off the debts with money they make from their jobs every month because the income from the properties doesn't support the loan payments they have to make! The couple now believes there was fraud involved, and is in the process of hiring an attorney that can help represent their case – and hopefully get some of their money back!

Unfortunately, it's not just U.S. companies coming to Canada and making a mess of things. Later in this chapter, I'll tell you a story about a course we attended at the end of 2012 given by a well known Canadian.

So that side of the industry isn't changing fast enough in my mind, but the good news is that *you* are changing and *the internet* is changing. A quick search on your favorite search engine or a shout out on Twitter or Facebook will reveal what people *really* think about what is being taught. It is up to YOU to do that research.

That, to me, is really exciting.

It means that the people who have tremendous value to offer and want to help their fellow investors will rise to the top, while the ones who are solely in the business to sell courses and make money will be pushed out.

It also means that real information will begin to be more influential than the promises of fast money.

Part of this problem lies with the student rather than the teacher. *You* must be aware of what you want to create in your life. You also need to ask good questions of yourself and of the people who are teaching. *Many things are possible, but are they probable?*

Getting support and coaching is a great way to save time, money and energy and avoid making mistakes along the way. But not all coaching and support out there is equal, nor is any one program the right solution for every real estate investor.

That's where this book is going to help you. You'll be able to ask yourself the right questions to ensure you do deals that move you closer to the life you want to live. And you'll be much better equipped to evaluate the coaching and courses you may want to take.

It may also scare you away from doing real estate deals you might otherwise have done – but that's good. I'd rather scare you away than entice you into thinking that real estate is always a massive money maker – because sometimes it's really crappy – and I do mean *really* crappy.

And sometimes it *is* a massive money maker … our biggest pay day to date was a cheque for $288,000. That's $288,000 before tax but after all other expenses. Not bad. It also took eight years and a lot of stress to get to that payday.

BACK TO THE REAL ESTATE INVESTING COURSE....

It's not that the get-rich-quick course teachings didn't work. In the year after the course – as they promised we could – we bought a handful of properties for little to no money down. For a while, they even put a lot of money in our pockets – but we were not in any way equipped to handle the challenges these properties presented. We didn't even know what issues to watch out for.

The crack house incident that put Dave's name in the local

newspaper was just one of many things that happened in the years after we had taken the courses.

When the article ran in the paper, we were still in the middle of dealing with the fact that our property manager in charge of that sixplex, and another triplex we owned in the same area, was being charged with manslaughter.

He was involved in an altercation with an aggressive tenant at another property and punched him. The tenant fell to the ground and hit his head on the cement, and later that night he died in the hospital. It was a tragic series of events and it was absolutely horrible for everyone involved.

We had to write pleading letters to the courts to allow our property manager (who had a curfew until his court hearing) out in the evening to handle tenant issues; he was the only guy who would do the job. Unfortunately, he spiraled further and further into depression while he was awaiting his trial and he was soon no longer able to work at all.

We were losing over $1,000 a month on those two properties due to vacancies. And, although we didn't know it yet, another property manager at a triplex we owned in a different city was robbing rent money from us.

If it weren't for the fact that we both had decent paying jobs, these disastrous investments could have forced us into bankruptcy. Even worse, the series of events was taking it's toll on our relationship, and we broke up for a while, and almost ended our relationship forever.

LIES, DANGEROUS TACTICS AND OTHER THINGS TO WATCH OUT FOR AT SOME REAL ESTATE INVESTING COURSES

A few years ago Dave and I attended a *real estate investing club meeting* in Langley, British Columbia. We went for many reasons ... the biggest ones being that we like to meet like-minded people, we wanted to meet the man behind the club, and we wanted to find answers to some questions about sandwich leases.

The feature presentation was from a local area mortgage broker who did an excellent job of explaining the important things you need to understand about mortgages as a real estate investor.

When we got to the part where we started discussing credit scores, the mortgage broker mentioned a couple he had just tried to find financing for. He noted that they had a bad credit score because they had 16 credit cards.

He went on to explain why having so many credit cards can be very damaging to your credit and how you should keep it to five, max. He also gave some other great tips, like keeping your credit card limit *high* but always keeping the amount you owe *low* because your credit will be negatively impacted with balances that are close to your limit.

At this point, one of the new real estate investors in the room raised her hand. She said, *"I just took a real estate investing course that told us to go out and get as many credit cards as possible. They said that having all that credit was a good thing."*

I actually felt Dave shudder beside me. That brought back memories of the real estate investing courses *we* had taken early on as investors. And it reminded us of the kind of advice that causes so much damage that it can take years to recover (as it did with us). We knew instantly that the speaker was referring to one of the big name courses that had come through town recently.

Even more incredible and potentially harmful was the fact that the woman didn't seem to believe the mortgage broker when he explained why this was horrible advice. She tried to argue: *"Well, you're not necessarily going to use the cards; you're just supposed to have them in case you need cash for a quick flip."*

Here are some of the high risk things we were taught at a *get-rich-quick type program* and the motive behind the lesson:

You must have a triple-tiered corporation – and you are stupid and foolish if you don't have one. *They actually used these words*, explaining all the horrible risks and extra taxes we'd pay if we didn't have one. Um … I guess we're beyond stupid because we bought a two-tiered corporation. The three-tiered one seemed like overkill, but we foolishly thought the two-tiered one made perfect sense. However, we were not able to buy and finance a single property in that fancy-pants $3,000 corporation the guru sold us – and we tried for three years!

Call your credit card company and demand a lower interest rate and higher balance on your credit card. Conveniently they got us to do this during our lunch break. We did as we were told – and by gosh – we were successful. It's a good thing too because thanks to that call we had $20,000 of available credit on our card that we could use to finance the big mentorship package they convinced us to buy at the end of the weekend. And, they assured us that with one deal we'd pay it off, so why not?! *By the way, it actually took us over a year to pay it off and then two more years to fix all the problems we created for ourselves by buying several troublesome high-leverage properties.*

Wholesaling, assignments, and sandwich leases are going to lead to tons of juicy and gigantic cheques within weeks of learning the techniques. These were hot topics at the course because cash always looks much juicier than a "boring old buy and hold" that takes years to produce super riches. Yes, one good assignment or wholesaling deal *can* give you a nice juicy cheque, but guess what – you aren't going to find that deal a week or two after the course because there are still a lot of things you have to learn before you can do that first deal. Luckily, before you leave the program, they help you to realize there are many more details you need to know before you can do *those* deals – *and* they offer just the solution – specific courses on each subject for $3,000-4,000 each so you can go out and learn more.

Listen – we fell for every one of those promises, so don't feel bad if you did too. These folks are master marketers. *If there's one thing the get-rich-quick courses do know how to do – it's sell!* We were determined to be successful real estate investors, so we believed what they said and dove head first into everything they had to offer.

It's a good thing we were determined or we would never have picked ourselves up and gone on to succeed after the early mistakes.

We struggled to fix the mess we got ourselves into, and it took us years! It wasn't until we invested in the *right* mentors and courses that we finally got great systems into place and made big things happen in our business.

Educating yourself is smart, but watch out for the get-rich-quick schemes and *watch for the lies you could be telling yourself!* Look for the people who are genuinely trying to help and someone who presents the realistic side of the story. I look for teachers who are upfront about risks, and about the time and the effort you need to invest in order to succeed. I also look for people who are teaching *fundamental principles* as well as their particular spin on investing. And most importantly, I want to know what else they might be selling in advance; so if they tell me I should invest in Florida, I know whether they are saying that because they also happen to sell investment properties in Florida or because they like the market fundamentals. It's okay either way, but I want to understand their bias. For instance, if they say I need a three-tiered corporation, I want to know whether it's because they are going to upsell me their package for a three-tiered corporation or whether it's because it actually saved them from losing everything in a law suit.

Think carefully about what you *need* to learn. If that course will give you what you need, then go. Before you sign up for *anything* additional that is being offered, think about the bias that might be behind what they are teaching. **And question what they are saying.**

CHAPTER TWO

THE BIGGEST MYTHS IN REAL ESTATE

There's a lot of crap being passed off as truth in real estate, but some of these supposed truths really mess people up – and they really messed us up.

Here are the five "truths" that came the closest to destroying us emotionally and financially:

1. Real estate investing gives you passive income.
2. Once you own a certain number of properties you'll be successful.
3. It's all about the numbers.
4. To reduce risk, you need to have a corporation (and you want to control real estate without being on the hook for it).
5. Real estate investing is easy.

The one that came the closest to destroying us emotionally and financially was the idea that real estate investing gives you passive income.

I'll cover all of these, along with a few others, before we get to the end of the book; but for now I want to focus on the one that most people hold most dearly … that is, *the belief that real estate investing is passive.*

But first let me contradict myself … it *can* be passive. And it can actually work out pretty well for you, but *someone* on your team has to be *active* and I'm not talking about a property manager.

From my experience, the *only* way it can be passive is if you work with an active investor who is going to oversee the property from purchase to disposition – and *everything* in between. If you have money to invest and can qualify for financing at the bank, you are in a good position to find someone with expertise, experience and energy to find, negotiate and oversee your investment. In that case, and *only* in that case, does real estate investing come close to being passive. Of course, you must give up some of the return in order to enjoy that scenario. Our JV Partners own the property 50 - 50 percent with us. After their initial investment in the deal (which is usually equivalent to the down payment + closing costs + 3 months of mortgage payment reserve), we split all profits and expenses. They give up equity to become passive, but most of our JV partners can make 15% or more each year on their money. It's much more than they make on the majority of their other investments, and they can do it without learning anything about real estate or ever handling a troubled tenant call.

Our JV partners spend some time at the beginning of the relationship doing due diligence on us, doing a little paperwork, and signing a cheque. Once that is done, it really is passive.

For us – and anyone else that is not just writing a cheque – it's *active*.

It's not full time, but it's active. So that's it. If you are the silent money partner in a deal you can be passive … other than that, *passive income is a myth.*

When I started investing in real estate in 2001, I had two main objectives: 1) get my money working hard for me so I didn't always have to work hard for my money; and 2) create multiple streams of passive income.

The problem with pursuing the goal of "passive income" is that you're telling yourself you don't have to do any work to make that money.

Keith Cunningham, author of *Keys to the Vault* says, "The label becomes the experience. Using the word 'passive' for anything means that you are going to do the least to get the most."

That might sound like a great idea, but the problem is that *trying to build wealth through passive income is like trying to get six-pack abs without working out.* It isn't going to happen. You can't do nothing and expect to get positive results.

When you buy a property, hire a property manager, and then do nothing more than deposit the rent money into your bank account, you're setting yourself up for trouble. We know!

We bought into the idea that we *could* get rich by finding properties to buy for no money down. We worked hard to find the properties, bought them, and then passively let things fall apart!

COULD YOUR PROPERTY MANAGER BE ROBBING YOU?

I was doing my MBA at the Schulich School of Business at York University in Toronto. When I walked out of the classroom after an intense three-hour lecture, I checked my cell phone. I had 23 missed calls and 18 voicemails. My stomach jumped. I figured someone must have died; why else would someone be so intense about calling?

I scrolled through the missed calls and most of them were from my tenant at a Triplex we owned. Maybe there was a fire at the house? That would explain all the calls....

About four months before, we had purchased a property in the Little Italy area of Toronto. It was our fifth investment purchase (and our third after the guru course). The difference between this one and the others was that it was the first one that we had decided to manage ourselves. Our rationale was simply that we lived close enough to this one to oversee it; it would cash flow better if I managed it; and my schedule was fairly flexible given that I was doing my MBA full time. Plus, we agreed I could take a management fee out of the cash flow for my efforts, and as a student I really needed the cash.

Once we completed the purchase, I read up on what I should do to manage the property, met with the tenants, had new leases signed, made a repair list, and got to work on making the tenants happy within our budget.

Things went okay for a few months but then one of the two guys downstairs moved out and the remaining guy wanted to get a new roommate. The new roommate checked out, so we updated the paperwork and he moved in. But he was a smoker and soon the problems began.

The upstairs tenant claimed he was smoking in the house and it was bothering her son's asthma. We asked the tenant to smoke outside, as per the lease, and he did. He also began harassing the son when he'd come home from school, calling him a tattletale and other not so nice names.

I was getting a couple of calls a day from the tenants and it was stressful. I didn't want to mediate their problems; I had problems of my own – specifically, I was struggling to pass a financial accounting class.

As the weather got colder and the downstairs tenants tried new and creative ways to smoke outside while remaining mostly indoors, the tension between the tenants increased to where it was the day that I received the 23 voicemails. Turns out the tenants had called the cops on each other! The fighting and threats had reached such a level that they were now involving the Toronto Police!

My final exams were a week away and the stress was just too much. I cracked. I wasn't sleeping; I was crying over any little thing; and I could barely eat. It was great for weight loss, but not so good for studying or getting anything important done.

So Dave hurried out and hired a property manager to take over from me. He found some options online, checked the better business bureau and a few references, and then grabbed the best priced guy he could find. The property manager took over, the calls stopped, and life got easier.

I let myself totally forget we owned the property. I swear I would drive by and look the other way. I finished school and looked for a job; I was no longer a property manager.

UNCOVERING THE SCAM

Fast forward about a year and a half. Two of the units in the triplex were about to be vacant, and the property needed some serious upgrading. A friend of ours was looking for a place to live and said he'd move in to the top unit if we moved in to the main floor. We offered him a very good rent rate in exchange for his support in the renovations (which at times meant we were actually cooking and using the bathroom in his unit and vice versa). He agreed and we all moved in and dismissed the property manager.

We started collecting rent from the other tenants directly. Imagine our surprise when the cheques were for $100 more than we expected! The property manager had lied to us about the amount of rent we were getting, and he had been pocketing the difference. He was probably doing this for all three units since all three leases had turned over since he'd taken over.

We also discovered maintenance issues that we had paid for but that were never fixed. We also began to suspect we'd been charged for snow removal on days when it hadn't snowed.

We figure he stole at least $2,000 from us in that one year; we had *passively* let him steal money from us!

Besides the fact that you should never hire a property manager just because their rate is the best you can find, you also should only hire based on a referral from someone you trust (if possible). No matter who you hire, stay *actively* involved in your property so something similar doesn't happen to you.

It's not a full time job but it's not passive. Ask for copies of every lease agreement, and ask for photocopies of the cheques. If the tenant pays by cash or some other method (we use a lot of e-mail money transfers with our tenants), get a printout of the transfer or get copies of the receipts given to the tenants for cash payments. It's good to have this documentation for tax purposes... and it will help prevent your property manager from taking an extra cut off the top.

AND ONE MORE STORY BECAUSE
PASSIVE INCOME IS A HARD BELIEF TO SHAKE

> *Beware of little expenses. A small leak will sink a great ship.*
> *~ Benjamin Franklin*

Believing in passive income caused us enough grief for me to fill this entire book with horror stories (don't worry – I won't do that to you – I have good stories too!).

I know you're smarter than we were, but I want to share *one more* story.

Ditching the belief that there is passive income in real estate *single-handedly made us more money and reduced our problems dramatically and almost instantly.*

By sharing our experience, I want to save you time and make you more money faster.

Looking back, it's astonishing how much money we left behind in expenses we paid that we shouldn't have; how much income we should have made but didn't; and how many problems we could have extinguished when there was smoke, instead of when the fire had consumed a large portion of our profits.

Here's just one example of how being actively involved saved us big time a few years ago.

Every month Dave does a review of the expense and income statements for each of our properties. Because he does this every month, anomalies are easier for him to spot. In this one property, Dave noticed the water bill was double what it usually was.

He immediately contacted our property manager and asked that it be checked out. The property manager said it was because the billing frequency had decreased. We were now being billed fewer times, so it was expected that our bills would be double when we were billed.

Because we owned properties in four different cities at that time, Dave wasn't sure if that was the case, but he seemed to remember that change had occurred over a year ago. He pulled up our property expense tracking spreadsheet – and sure enough – we'd moved to bi-monthly billing over a year ago.

He called our property manager back and insisted that he investigate.

Turns out we had a water leak. The leak was quickly fixed and the next water bill was back to normal. This home is a split level with a one-bedroom basement suite, and because the tenants aren't on separate water meters we pay those bills. Dave's swift action saved us hundreds of dollars that year, not just from wasted water but also because he minimized the damage to the home by catching the leak sooner!

It wouldn't take too many little leaks like this to completely remove all the cash flow from this property.

So besides just monitoring the water bills ... what else should you watch for with your rental property?

Rent payments: If you're managing the property yourself, you'll typically notice when you haven't been paid; but when you have a property manager handling your rent collection, you might forget about it. You also might assume your property manager will let you know if rent has not been paid, but that is not always the case. Stay on it. If the rent wasn't paid, find out why and what's been done to address the matter. Never assume things are being handled. In every case, a non-payment-of-rent notice (or the equivalent type of notice for your state or province) should be issued, in case you eventually have to take steps to evict the tenant.

Utility bills: Whether you pay the utilities or not, you

should keep an eye on the bills because increased utilities could indicate other issues, as in the case of the water leak. It could also indicate a broken seal on a window or a door if your heating or cooling costs have gone up ... or just inconsiderate energy usage. When our tenants usage of electricity goes up more than 25%, we always let them know and remind them to turn lights off, turn the heat down, turn off the TV when not in use, and so on. It's not just better for our bottom line; it's better for the environment.

Repairs and maintenance: Your property managers should be getting three quotes for any major work. If it's going to cost you more than $500 to do something, you need options. And you need to insist on this.

You also need to monitor what is going on. Unfortunately, we have many examples of where our property managers mismanaged repairs and maintenance, not obtained more than one quote, or allowed the repair budget to go well over the amount we agreed upon. Even with diligent management, we still have these issues on a regular basis; and sometimes we don't have enough time to deal with it ourselves so we spend money that we could have saved.

Listen to the warnings of Ben Franklin and watch out for those small "leaks." Spend a few hours every month reviewing your expenses and cash flow. Ideally, enter them into a tracking program or a spreadsheet so the discrepancies are easy to spot.

So what about financial freedom and buying enough property so you never have to worry about money again?

Let's say you do the math ... you figure out that owning 30 properties that make you $300/month positive income will allow you to quit your job. And if you can quit your job, you will have financial freedom! Finally!

What a romantic load of crap that is!

What *is* financial freedom anyway? Most people try to convince me that it's never worrying about money again. If that is financial freedom, you aren't going to get there with real estate. "More properties" does not equal more freedom ... more properties equals more roofs that leak, more appliances that break, more hot water tanks that flood, and a whole lot more tenants to deal with. Even if you have the best team, these things will still require your attention – and I assure you that during the week you're trying to finally relax you will have a tenant move out on short notice – leaving you with a property to fix up, a hot water tank split open, and a plumber that seems to have vanished off the face of the earth. And these kinds of situations don't space themselves out nicely – they all happen at once. The expression "When it rains it pours" was not created because of the weather!

Let's be clear on one thing: "Financial freedom" is bogus. It doesn't really mean anything. It's a fluffy phrase that sounds wonderful but doesn't translate into any kind of reality.

And real estate is NOT the way to go if you never want to worry about money again. More properties is just that ... more properties.

THE LIES THAT MAKE THE REAL ESTATE WORLD GO ROUND

I'm bashing real estate education a bit – and I'm not quite done. But again I want to emphasize that education is *smart*. We've invested more than $100,000 in training and coaching, and we continue to put five figures into our education every single year. We believe there is no other investment that can give you the kind of returns you get from the right kind of training and coaching. Period.

But many people find themselves in courses – as well as deals and partnerships – that don't work. And that happens because of myths and lies.

Let me tell you a story about myths and lies in the real estate business and also share the seven biggest lies that we tell ourselves.

Tears welled up in my eyes as I watched at least 20 people in their fifties and sixties rush to surround the back table. Watching so many men my dad's age waiting with their credit cards in hand made me feel uncharacteristically emotional. I could sense them struggling to fund their retirement, worrying about helping their kids, and believing that the things they would learn at this three-day $1,997 seminar would somehow have the solution. I felt helpless. Basically, we had just been lied to several times by the presenter who had come to our hometown of Nanaimo, BC to offer this free lunchtime session on real estate investing.

The presenter got everyone excited by sharing a testimonial from an American fellow who had taken their seminar at the beginning of 2011. This guy had been living in a 300-square-foot apartment and working in a machine shop. After the seminar, he did 350 deals, moved into a fancy condo, and bought his first car – a Lamborghini – with the cash he'd made in real estate. The presenter even showed a picture of the guy with his new car. "Sure, he worked hard," the presenter acknowledged, "but this is possible."

Someone in the audience asked when exactly the guy had taken the seminar – undoubtedly thinking this just didn't seem possible – and the presenter reiterated that it was at the start of 2011.

I didn't believe it for a second, so I pulled out my iPhone and googled the name of the guy from the testimonial. The good news was that the story wasn't totally made up; their guy was an active real estate investor. The bad news was that he'd been an investor for many years and had built up a lot of deals since taking a different program in 2005 (not 2011). His profile was on a real estate website that told his whole story. He'd been investing since 2005, quit his job in 2008, and already owned 50 rentals well before 2011.

This wasn't the only thing that was inaccurately presented. The presenter defined a subprime mortgage as "a mortgage the banks gave to someone they knew could never pay it back." By leaving out a few critical details, he also made it sound like you would make between $20,000 and $63,000 per wholesale deal – when, in fact, it would be closer to $5,000.

Despite the lies and mixed messages, it was a very different sales pitch from some of the guru pitches of the past. He came across as pleasant and genuine; there was no pressure; the price was the price and there were no price-slashing gimmicks.

It worked like a charm.

I commend the folks for taking action and signing up for courses to help them get started. My issue is not that people were pulling out their credit cards to educate themselves; my issue is what took place in order for this sales pitch to work.

The reality is that pitches like this one work not just because of the lies told by the presenter, but because of the lies we tell ourselves.

The folks rushing to be the ones that would have their travel and hotel costs covered to attend the seminar in Vancouver were likely telling themselves all kinds of lies to believe that it could, in fact, be that easy – and as lucrative as promised.

Great things *are* possible. Exceptions happen; and if you're an active investor, you just might enjoy a few exceptions in your career. *But exceptions are not the norm.* You can't *expect* to be an exception, and you have to understand that it's going to be way more work than you think and take longer than you estimate.

As real estate investors, new or experienced, there are a lot of lies we tell ourselves that mess us up in a big way. Sometimes we end up in courses that are useless or worse; other times we end up in a bad deal or a bad partnership. And sometimes the lies we tell ourselves can land us an entire portfolio of problems we hadn't planned for.

The worst part is that we don't even know we're lying to ourselves – which makes it even more dangerous. So what lies do you need to watch out for?

Here are seven common lies that many real estate investors tell themselves about what they *can't* do and what they *can* do.

WHAT YOU THINK YOU CAN'T DO:

---

1. I CAN'T SELL / I'M HOPELESS AT SELLING.

Even if you're not in real estate, you're in sales. Everyone sells every day. If you want to eat at your favorite restaurant, you may have to sell others on the idea. When you negotiate bed time with your kids or leaving work early with your boss – you're selling. Whether you realize it or not – you *are* a salesperson.

You use your powers of influence to get the results you want in so many areas of your life – and most of the time you do this unconsciously. So accept that you already use tactics to influence others and make conscious choices to improve your skills in influencing or selling. Or you can continue to believe you can't sell and wonder why you aren't getting the results you want.

2. I JUST NEED ... ONE MORE COURSE ... ONE MORE BOOK ... TO LOOK AT MORE PROPERTIES ... ETC., AND THEN I CAN DO IT.

The harsh truth about this is that you probably don't need *anything* else; you just don't have enough faith in yourself to do it. You're lacking confidence and that has you hanging on to the feeling that it's just because you're missing something. If you truly are missing something, go out and get it. However, if you're clinging to the notion that you *just need* something before you can finally do what you know you need to do, then the only thing left to do is STOP.

Real estate investing is scary, but it's also forgiving. You don't have to be perfect in order to make money and build your wealth. However, you'll never make any money if you're sitting on the sidelines.

3. "BUT YOU ARE LUCKY...."

Want to know one of the easiest ways to get on my nerves fast? Suggest that something cool is happening in my world because I am *lucky*.

I've had people say "Yeah, but you're lucky ... because it's easier when you don't have kids" or "...because you and your husband don't have full-time jobs anymore" or "...because you're in the Canadian Real Estate Wealth Magazine all the time."

Part of the reason it irritates me is because it discounts all the time, effort and energy I've put into getting to where I am today. Maybe it looks like luck, but it's *far* beyond luck. Both my husband and I have worked hard and made some tough decisions and persevered when we've gotten off on the wrong track – and you'll know exactly what I mean by the time you've finished this book.

The bigger reason it makes me mad is that the individuals saying these things have completely discounted their own strengths and abilities, and therefore excused themselves from achieving success. They are blaming something else in their lives for the reason they aren't the person they want to be, when the only thing they should look at is themselves!

The word "lucky" lets them believe that it's luck that has put those of us who have achieved success in the position we're in; not years of hard work, years of investing money instead of spending it, and years of making hard choices that eventually opened the door of opportunity for us to leave our jobs and begin living a more freedom-filled life. If you're telling yourself that you can't do what someone else is doing because they were *lucky* – you're lying to yourself.

---

4. REAL ESTATE INVESTING IS PASSIVE.

We had two property managers rob rent money from us in our first five years as real estate investors. Do you wonder how that could happen? Believe me; it happens quite easily when you believe that your income from real estate is *passive*.

Passive income is a terrible phrase to use because it tells your brain you can get something for doing *nothing*. When is that ever really the case?

The reality is that *nobody* ever loves your money like you do! You need to stay actively involved, ask questions, verify expenses, double check revenue, and pay attention to your team, the market, and your property.

If you do that, you'll minimize surprises and actually make some money. If you don't do that, you might wake up one day realizing your property manager has $2000 of your hard-earned rent because he has been collecting $100 more per month on each unit than he's been telling you.

5. EVEN IF IT LOSES A BIT OF MONEY EVERY MONTH, AT LEAST IT'S A TAX DEDUCTION.

When we were looking for our first investment property, some key people on our team and in our circle of influence at the time basically said, "It's hard to find a property that makes money every month. Don't worry about it. You have jobs, so you don't need to add income and pay more tax. If you lose money every month, it's a write-off anyway – so don't worry about it."

There are two harsh realities to this statement. The first is that you won't be able to own very many properties if they all lose money every month.

The second is that just because you're losing money every month does *not* mean it's a tax write-off. You cannot write off the mortgage principal pay down in Canada – and it is usually one of the largest expenses you have every month.

If, on the other hand, you're investing in the U.S., the rules are different; so check with your accountant to make sure you understand what you can and can't write off. One great guy to check with is Bill Walston. Drop him a note on his blog at www.billonbusiness.net and he'll be happy to help you out.

Whether you're in Canada or the U.S. you can write off the interest on your mortgage, and you can write off the insurance, taxes, management and repairs. But just because your revenue is $1200/month and your expenses are $1375 doesn't mean you will have a $175 loss to write off. In most cases, you won't.

6. IF THAT PERSON CAN DO IT, I CAN TOO.

Sometimes this is true. However, all too often this is based on very limited information.

The fact that the guy from the testimonial did 350 deals in 2011 may look like proof that it can be done. You may even think something like "if he can do 350 in one year, I can certainly do 5!"

However, you missed out on the information that he'd already been doing it for five years before that. You don't know how big of a team he has, or what price he has paid to do that. How is his health? What are his relationships like? Is he happy? Is he honest? And frankly, what exactly are his rentals doing for him? Just because somebody has 110 rentals doesn't mean he's making money!

You don't know any of that information. If you did have all the details, you may not want to do what he did at all. His life may look nothing like how you want your life to be.

7. NO PROBLEM – WE CAN MAKE IT WORK.

Underestimating expenses, overestimating potential rent, ignoring maintenance, and thinking you can manage it yourself to save money, are all things you might be telling yourself in order to make the numbers work.

The problem is that you're usually wrong.

If it's a good deal – it's a good deal. If it's not a good deal, you'll have to try to convince yourself that "you can make it work," when what you should really be doing is looking for a better deal.

Good marketing and the right improvements can increase the rent. There are a few things you can do to reduce the expenses you have on a property, like shop your insurance around, improve the energy efficiency, and reward tenants for taking care of snow removal or lawn care. Managing a property yourself can save money, but what if you aren't very good at it, or you end up unable to handle it and have to hire a property manager? It's prudent to always factor property management costs into your deal analysis, even if you're planning to manage it yourself; because you never know when something might happen to cause that to change (moving, new job responsibilities, twin babies, sick parent, etc.).

There are a lot of things that make a good deal, but it's not the things you think you can do "to make it work."

It's often more difficult to lie to other people than it is to lie to yourself. I've lied to myself many times. When I have, I've found myself signing up for courses that weren't the right fit for my goals, agreeing to deals I didn't really want to do, and trying to do deals that weren't going to work.

Don't feel bad if you can relate to any of these lies. We are brilliant at deceiving ourselves, and I haven't met an investor yet that hasn't lied to himself or herself at least a few times in their career.

My hope is that by sharing these common lies with you, you'll at least recognize them when they pop up in front of you! I also hope that it will make you think twice before rushing into deals, courses or relationships that aren't going to help you create the life you want from real estate.

CHAPTER THREE

HOW TO BECOME A FULL-TIME REAL ESTATE INVESTOR – EVEN THOUGH YOU MIGHT NOT ACTUALLY WANT TO BE ONE

W hen I announced my intention to quit my job, my friends thought it was cool until I couldn't afford to go for dinner or travel to their weddings or gatherings anymore. A few friends stuck by me and were supportive; but most didn't get it, tried to pressure me, and then stopped inviting me to social events and get-togethers.

Most of my family was supportive and believed we could make it work. I know it scared the heck out of my Grandpa Broad though. "Why would you leave such a high paying job? You're going to get another job, right?" he asked me. Then darn near every time I talked to him until he passed away he'd ask me, "Did you make any money today?" I would always find creative ways to explain that we were making progress but that great things don't happen overnight. I tried to be positive when I was with him, but there were days where I was faking it, and when I wondered if we could keep pushing to make it happen.

We'd been used to living on my six-figure salary so we had to make changes and sacrifices and redirect what cash we had toward the growth of our income.

It was only two months after I had left my job when it became painfully obvious that we couldn't maintain our Burnaby home mortgage payments, car payments and other high expenses and still have the cash resources we needed to be able to grow the business. I told Dave that something had to go so we could make it work: the house or the car.

He chose the house. It would reduce the biggest expense and we had options; so we turned our home into a furnished rental and moved in with my mom and dad.

Maybe it's not where every newlywed couple dreams of spending the first few years after marriage, but we made it work – and my parents were gracious hosts while we moved in and out for almost two years until we were fully on our feet and could buy an amazing home and office to live and work from.

Very few people are willing to do what we did. It wasn't just that we moved in with my mom and dad; we turned our home, complete with all our stuff, into a furnished rental. The market wasn't good when we needed to make the change, so selling it wouldn't have been a wise move. The costs were too high to be covered by a regular rental so a furnished rental was the only thing that made complete financial sense. I had tenants sleeping in my bed, using the dishes that we got as a gift for our wedding, and wearing their dirty work boots in my house!

Like I said, many people wouldn't be willing or able to do what we did to make it work for us.

HOW MUCH INCOME DO YOU NEED TO GO FULL TIME?

It was as though he had come face to face with a 600 lb grizzly bear in the wild. My coaching client was so scared his voice actually shook as he spoke.

I make an average of about $200 per month per property for the three properties I own. Based on that and the prices around here, I need to buy $5,610,000 worth of real estate to replace my salary. But I only have $40,000 left to invest, so I don't see how that is going to be possible.

I couldn't help but laugh because that *did* sound scary.

Thankfully, I never did that kind of math or I never would have left the cushy six-figure salary and vice-president title I had for the not-so-glamorous life of a real estate investor.

I never calculated what I'd have to make to replace the benefits package I would be giving up or the paid vacation time I was walking away from. If I had figured it out like that, I would likely have been paralyzed with fear, and I certainly would not have dragged my husband out of his job to join me.

If I had thought that way, I would have missed out.

Quitting my job was the best decision I've ever made. It was also one of the hardest things I've ever done.

I wasn't mentally or financially ready to leave when I made the leap. And the real estate market was in shambles; it was the fall of 2008. There were a dozen reasons why it was not the right time to leave.

But the moment arrived when I had been disappointed and disheartened one too many times in my job. I am not one to complain and do nothing about the problem. I was unhappy, so I either had to change jobs or take the leap into real estate full time.

I didn't even consider finding another job.

I called my husband Dave and told him I was going to quit my job. Probably not the words he wanted to hear when he was a new mortgage broker trying to make a living in an ugly housing market – but he took it like a champ.

We tightened our belts and cut expenses. We gave up planned vacations and visits with friends that would cost us money. And I started working harder than I ever had before.

It was not easy, and even today I have days when it's really difficult, but I have to tell you that I am *so happy* that I didn't wait to quit my job.

Dave and I are five times stronger financially than we would have been if I had stayed in my job! We have conquered challenges in the last few years that astound us! And because Dave joined me full time shortly after I left my job, we made all the big leaps side by side.

The greatest thing we gained was the time and energy to *focus*. In one single month we are able to dedicate the same amount of energy to our real estate business that we could have in an entire *year* when we were both working full time. That focus alone has multiplied the quality and quantity of our network, amplified our ability to do more deals, and vastly increased our energy for what we're doing!

And even cooler for me is that I am now spending a huge portion of my days writing and teaching. That is what gets me excited – seeing people make massive leaps, gain confidence, and look at their business and lives differently is *hugely rewarding*.

Most days I like real estate, but I *love* helping, teaching and inspiring others. Real estate has opened those doors for me, but I am the one that jumped through them.

Now ... I'm not saying run out and quit your job today because it's the best thing ever. I refuse to write about becoming a full time investor without warning you that the life of a full time real estate investor is not for everyone.

In fact, for many people I think leaving their job for real estate would be a big mistake. Maybe you just need a different job?

There is *nothing* wrong with having a job. For many it offers stability, comfort and satisfaction, and that's good.

Yet, amongst the real estate community, there sometimes seems to be something like shame in having a job. People even spell it out like it's a swear word, saying I have to leave my "J-O-B."

Personally, I think there is shame in living a life that makes you miserable. I think there is shame in complaining about your life and doing nothing to make it better. But I do not think there is shame in having a job, and some people love their job. They are smart ... they use their job to help them buy great real estate so their children's education and their financial future are taken care of. They don't, however, worry about the fact they have a job; they are proud of it.

But if you long for freedom like I did, this book will help you become a full time real estate investor. But you have to be practical. We all have to eat and we all need shelter. When I quit, we'd already built up a multi-million dollar portfolio and a net worth in excess of $1,000,000.

The challenge we faced was that *you can't eat equity.* Our cash flow wasn't high enough to feed and shelter us anywhere near the way we'd been living when we had salaries.

And from the day I made the decision to quit, it was still six months before I actually left. We made preparations to reduce our expenses, save more money and learn more about strategies to increase our cash flow. *The final decision happened instantly, but the actual event took time and preparation.*

PREPARING FOR "THE BIG LEAP"

Whether you're on your first deal or seven years into it like we were when I quit my job, here's what you'll need to do to get ready....

1. GET CLEAR ON THE MONEY YOU'RE SPENDING NOW.

First, you will need to take an honest look at where you are financially. If you don't know exactly what you're spending each month, figure that out. Track it for at least three months.

I also recommend that you reduce your expenses as much as possible to prepare for the switch. It's stressful enough stepping out on your own; you don't need thousands of dollars in debt payments each month to make it worse.

I *don't* recommend that you calculate how to replace your income. *Instead, I recommend that you take a look at your expenses each month and figure out what you need to make each month to live on.*

Real estate allows for a lot of write-offs. Things you would have normally paid for with your after-tax dollars you can now pay for with your before-tax dollars and then write it off against your income to further reduce the amount you need to make to live on.

You'll also find that you require less income when you're not working.

I easily saved $300-400 per month when I left my job because I stopped buying breakfast or lunch on the run. When I eat out now, it's often a tax write-off because it's business related.

I also saved a lot of money because I no longer wear suits that need dry cleaning, because I don't pay for parking or transit passes, and because I don't need as many massages, pedicures, or expensive dinners out as a reward for surviving a bad day at work! When you are excited about what you're doing, suddenly a lot of things you do just to get through the day are no longer necessary.

If you now have your kids in daycare full time, you will probably find you can cut that time back, and that will save you money and allow you to spend more time with your kids.

So figuring out how to replace the $85,000 per year you're making now isn't really the way to look at it; because the value of a dollar is different when it's income from a job versus money made through real estate. However, knowing what you need to make each month to live is critical.

2. CREATE A CASH-TODAY / CASH-TOMORROW PLAN.

Some investors will argue with me, but after more than eleven years of buy-and-hold investing, it's my opinion that it's *very* hard to live off the cash flow from buy-and-hold property unless you have the mortgages paid off.

Even when you have a positive-cash-flow buy-and-hold property, you'll generally find that on average it doesn't put much in your pocket. When a tenant moves out, you'll replace carpets, paint, and possibly even upgrade the bathroom or kitchen; and over time you'll have to replace a furnace or a roof. One year you might pocket a decent amount of money from the rental income, but then the next year you'll have to redo the deck or replace the hot water tank or paint the house, and you'll be pulling a few bucks out of your pocket to cover it. Unless you do the manual labor yourself (and trust me – the novelty of "sweat equity" wears off pretty quick when you have a handful of properties!); you will find that most properties won't net you more than a few thousand per year on average. You *will* have to own a lot of property to survive on just a few thousand per year per property.

What buy-and-hold lacks in cash today, it makes up for in cash tomorrow. Over time its value to you accelerates. The mortgage pays down faster and faster, and usually the appreciation grows year over year, on average. Ten years from now, that buy-and-hold property will be a beautiful bounty of cash if you need it.

So you have cash tomorrow figured out with buy-and-hold, but what about cash today?

There are a lot of ways to tackle this when you no longer have a job to cover cash today. What we did was add rent-to-own to our portfolio. It satisfied cash today because we would get the option fee (usually a $7,500 to $10,000 payment) upfront plus we would make better cash flow each month. Most of our rent-to-owns make us $600-$800 per month. The combination of the cash flow plus a deposit fee every time we completed another rent-to-own deal, boosted our income quickly to the point where we could comfortably live financially.

But there's more to this story than I will share in this chapter. I have an entire chapter dedicated to rent-to-own because it's certainly not a magic button to money. There is no magic button in life or real estate.

Some investors I know find deals and assign them to other investors for a fee. This is a transactional strategy and requires you to keep digging for deals – which is hard to do when you're working but is much more feasible when your time is free. You could also get into flipping houses. Ian Szabo has a great book entitled *From Renos to Riches* if you want to learn how to tackle renovations for profit.

Of course, many other investors end up getting their realtor's license to make money on their deals and other people's deals.

All of these strategies require ongoing labor, but they can give you more cash today to work with.

3. GET SUPPORT – LOTS OF SUPPORT.

I am assuming, at this point, that you already understand the fundamentals of real estate investing. You know how to do market research, you understand the real estate cycles, and you are comfortable finding and doing deals.

However, if you are unsure about any of that, you *must* get a foundation in those areas first. We're going to cover these areas in the upcoming chapters, but you'll need more expertise than I can offer in one single book.

But once you have that foundation, I believe the most important thing you can do is *build a massive support system around you.*

The single greatest factor in our success, over the four years since I left my job, has been the fact that we have hired great coaches to help us at each stage, and we have consciously chosen to surround ourselves with like-minded people. As our business grew, we invested a lot of time and money in our own personal growth, and we traveled the country to meet the best people that we could learn from. We have developed friendships with people all over North America who are doing cool and inspirational things in real estate and otherwise, so we are always supported, motivated and inspired to learn and develop our skills.

At a time when we were cutting back our expenses and trying to spend less, it seemed counterintuitive to spend $16,000 on masterminds and coaching. And it seemed risky to invest $5,000 to fly to San Diego for business conferences on marketing. *But those investments paid us back more than any investment we've ever made in real estate.*

We met so many people who supported us when we were struggling emotionally to get through tough spots. We hired coaches that guided us through obstacles and opportunities. We'll never know how much they saved us in mistakes but we can tell you that we *tripled* the number of deals we were able to do, and we raised more money in a year than we had in the previous five years. It made a huge difference to have good coaches and a strong network behind us.

If there is one thing we wish we would have done sooner, it's taking advantage of the benefits of good coaching and a strong network. In fact, this might be the first thing you choose to do, because the support of a great coach that has been where you want to go and a group of like-minded people to share the journey with will make the other steps easier too.

It's worth noting that the best coach for you probably won't be holding a free seminar at a hotel room near you. I'll share my thoughts on finding a great coach near the end of the book, but for now just know that the ideal coach for you is someone that spends time understanding you and your business goals, has been where you are, and isn't so far beyond where you're at now that he/she can no longer relate or understand what steps you need to take.

One of our coaching clients, Ryan, paid us $10,000 for a year of coaching. He hadn't yet done a deal, but he recognized that he'd easily save that money on his first deal with the help of third-party, unbiased advice, from experienced investors, coming his way at every step in the process. He then pointed out that every deal he did after that first one was just a bonus return on his investment.

WAIT – ARE YOU DRINKING THE KOOL-AID?
BEING A FULL TIME REAL ESTATE INVESTOR CAN SUCK

Buy-and-hold rental property is a critical component to every real estate portfolio. I think it is the greatest wealth creator over time. But if you want to live off your real estate without waiting to pay off the mortgages or working your butt off to buy 100 houses, then you'll need to find a way to bring in some cash *today*. *That's the kicker that not enough people talk about.*

Yes – the freedom of doing your own thing *can* be awesome. It can also end up being a lot more stressful than any job, and it can take over your life – day and night – in an all-consuming way that most jobs never do.

An interesting thing happened at a recent Investor Forum event. I found myself in a conversation with a rather verbally aggressive young fellow. He was in my face a bit, asking why we weren't buying multi-family property. In his mind, it was the symbol of success – likely because one of the speakers that day was on his way to his 3000ᵗʰ unit and tossed million-dollar stories around like they were Frisbees.

The attendee seemed to think that bigger was better, and that by sticking to what we were doing – buying single family homes – we were small time and not doing as well as we should be doing.

The point that was lost on him was one that was flashing in neon lights to Dave and myself: *There's a price for everything.*

The speaker who was buying so many multi-family properties actually admitted on stage that: "You just have to learn to get used to higher and higher levels of stress." He was basically confessing that he operates with a ton of stress.

We don't know him at all, but we've grown wise in our 11 years of investing adventures and we know that there is more to his story; we know that somewhere – maybe his marriage, his kids, his business or his health – he's paying a price. As long as it's a price he's okay to pay, that's his call. For me, the idea of getting used to higher and higher levels of stress doesn't sound healthy, and health is one of my highest values. If I'm not healthy, then what is the point of anything – because I won't be well enough to enjoy it!

Buying houses and renting them out – when done selectively over time – is pretty awesome. If you're using it to build your wealth so you can take a big around-the-world trip in ten years, send your kids to university, or pay for your retirement – and in the meantime you have good income from a job or a business – you're golden! Keep doing what you're doing.

If you want out of your job, or you're really committed to using real estate to create the life you want to live, then you can do that but I want you to know that you're still going to need another source of income.

You can try to get by without some other source of income, but it will be difficult. There are very few real estate investors that are living off their rental income only. We did for awhile but we also sold some properties to help us make all the payments and still enjoy life.

One thing that's important to realize is that there are ebbs and flows to the real estate cycle. At times you have to feed the business with cash. That means you need to make enough cash so that you can pay your bills *and* have some extra for the lean times when you need to kick in some cash to keep things rolling along smoothly.

FIVE STRATEGIES

Most real estate investors create their "cash today" using one of the following five strategies:

1. Wholesaling or assignments
2. Flipping
3. Becoming a realtor
4. Creating a property management business
5. Adding a strategy like rent-to-own that will increase your cash flow on a monthly basis. (This is what we did when I quit my job four years ago).

So what are these strategies? (Besides the perfect way to create a job for yourself that you probably don't really want....) *Do* stop to think about that. **Ultimately each of these options is a full time job or a business that you'll be creating for yourself.** If you're getting into real estate for freedom but you need to use one of these strategies to make money, just know that to do each of them successfully, you have to invest a lot of time, some money and give up that notion of total freedom for several years while you build up your business, systems and team to make that strategy work for you.

Here are the five "cash today" strategies:

1. WHOLESALING TO MAKE MORE CASH WITH REAL ESTATE

Wholesaling is basically where you do all the legwork to find under-market deals and get them under contract. Then you assign them to someone else for a fee.

Traditional wholesale models are where an investor just wants to be assigned a profit-producing property. You put in the effort to market, filter and negotiate the great deals and build a network of investors that will buy the deals from you, and then when you have a good deal you assign it to an investor.

This model is a great way to add thousands of dollars to your pocket for every deal you do. Of course, the challenge with wholesaling is that you always have to work your funnel of deals and build your investor network so you have supply and demand for the product. It is a lot of work – but it does help fill your bank account once you get your systems in place.

2. FLIPPING TO MAKE MORE CASH WITH REAL ESTATE

Most people think they know what it takes to flip a house, thanks to all the TV shows on the subject.

Ian Szabo, author of *From Renos to Riches* and creator of FlipSchool.ca, is a guy who knows what it takes to make $50,000 – $150,000 on a flip (he does two or three a year). He says he flips houses in two ways:

1. He buys a derelict house in a great area, fixes it up, and sells it for a juicy profit.
2. He buys a house that needs work, adds a legal suite, re-finances to pull out all his money and some profit, and then rents it out to make cash flow.

Flipping is a high-risk strategy, however, and even Ian doesn't recommend anyone approach it without a back-up strategy in place.

With the right strategy, the right house and the right plan, most flippers starting out can make about $30,000 on a flip, according to Ian. And that seems about right. Crystal, one of our coaching clients just did her first flip in 2012 and made pretty close to that.

With that kind of profit potential, you'd only need to do one or two a year to really fill in your "cash today" needs.

How easy is it to flip in a slow market? You have to do *really smart* deals, run tight renovations, and hope the market doesn't fluctuate down while you finish the work.

Flipping in a slump is stressful, just like doing rent to owns and being a realtor can be lean in a slump; so you have to consider that when you're relying on this as a strategy for your "cash today."

3. BECOMING A REALTOR TO MAKE MORE CASH WITH REAL ESTATE

I don't have an official survey or anything, but I'd venture to say this is one of the most common ways real estate investors make their "cash today." When you're an active buyer of real estate, and you watch your agent make $10,000 in commission for doing minimal work, you can't help but consider working as a realtor on your own deals. When you also realize that you can help a few of your investor friends and make a bit of commission on their deals too, it can be very appealing for you to become a realtor to satisfy your needs for "cash today." Plus you'll get access to all the MLS data for your area.

That said; *it is a distraction.* No matter how little you do as a realtor, it takes time and money just to have your license. We ruled it out because we decided it would distract us from our primary business, which is buying real estate. There are also some other challenges with being both a realtor and an investor, such as ensuring you follow disclosure rules and other licensed realtor requirements. Further, there can be considerable ongoing brokerage and marketing costs to stay licensed as a realtor.

For many investors, though, it's been the ticket to freedom. If you can stay focused on your investment business and build a successful side business as a realtor, it's a popular way for many real estate investors to make their "cash today."

4. CREATING A PROPERTY MANAGEMENT BUSINESS TO MAKE MORE CASH WITH REAL ESTATE

At one point, with property all over Canada, we were working with six different property management firms. When we quit our jobs and began to spend more time evaluating our cash flow, we began to spot a lot of cash leaks.

To plug some of the holes, we began bringing our property management efforts in-house. With the money we saved on property management expenses each month, we could afford to hire someone to help us. By doing most of our own property management, we find that we make more money every month and spend less money to do it.

Many other investors have come to this conclusion as well. And if they do their own property management well, their investor friends take notice and ask for help managing their properties.

But it takes a lot of work, and it's not exactly fast cash. You also should take note that some provinces require a Property Management license to manage properties that are not your own.

5. RENT TO OWN TO MAKE MORE CASH WITH REAL ESTATE

Rent to own is when a tenant rents your property with the option to purchase it. You set their purchase price at the beginning; they pay a fee for the option to purchase it in the future; and a portion of their rent is a credit that builds up over time towards their purchase.

It generates more cash flow because the tenants are paying a higher than market rent for their property in exchange for credits that build up towards their purchase, and they are responsible for basic maintenance. Also, you typically don't need property management because of the quality of tenants that move in and because they are responsible for taking care of repairs up to a certain dollar amount ($300 in our case, but many other investors have their tenants handle up to $500 or even $1,000).

When I quit my job, we evaluated all of the options for cash today. Wholesaling requires constant marketing and funnel management. If you're not constantly finding sellers and buyers, you aren't making money. Flipping is stressful and higher risk. It also requires you to be consistently working on a flip or you won't be filling your cash needs. We felt being a realtor would reduce the focus from our own deals and since we were planning to do a deal every month or so, we knew we'd need a lot of focus for that. And property management is not something we really enjoy, so we didn't want to create a business around it.

That left us with *rent to own* as the best solution for us.

By changing a few of our existing rentals to rent to own, and adding just a handful of rent to own properties to our portfolio, we were able to boost our cash – with the option fees and the increased cash flow – to a point where we were comfortable financially from our real estate holdings. We also like the fact that rent to own helps good people get into home ownership. Our rent to own tenants give us big warm hugs, invite us for dinner, make us handmade thank you cards, and invest in fixing up the homes.

We do have to continue to add properties in order to keep the cash flowing, because rent to own deals do turn over every 12 to 24 months after purchasing them. That has largely been the reason we have so aggressively added property to our portfolio in the last three years – around 10 to 12 new properties a year. But we like rent to own because if we want to take a month off from working on our deals, we still make money. *We can't say that about any of the other strategies.*

However, I'm not saying rent to own is a perfect strategy, and I'll explain why. You have to understand the real estate cycles and be careful about when you're offering rent to owns and how you are pricing them. If you are in a very hot market, you will end up selling your property for quite a bit less than you could have made, had you sold it on the market normally. On the other hand, in a market that is heading downwards, pricing a rent to own in a way that is fair to a tenant *and* that will still make you money is extremely difficult. And, even if the market in your area is doing okay; if the overall economic sentiment is poor, people will have a hard time believing the house will be worth the same as it is today, let alone slightly more. *Plus,* when the market is slow, both your business as a realtor and your rent to own business can dry right up.

We experienced this in 2012. The market in Nanaimo slowed down and all the news was doom and gloom around real estate in the Vancouver market. Then sales in the Nanaimo area dropped to levels not seen in a decade. How excited are people about signing a contract to rent to own a property, knowing they are committing to a *higher* price two years from now when everyone thinks prices are going to drop?

They aren't.

We had four rent to own deals – or properties that were supposed to be rent to owns – become rentals in 2012. If you want to do the math; that was approximately a $15,000-$20,000 drop in option fees for us (we have partners on all the deals) and about $1,200/month in cash flow that we lost as a result of these deals becoming rentals instead of rent to owns. Do you think that had an impact on our business? It didn't put us under because we are big enough now, but if this had happened in our second year it would have been devastating. As a result of these deals not working, we only bought six properties in 2012 instead of the planned 10. That is more income we aren't generating, but we felt it was prudent to minimize our exposure while the market was unsteady.

If we had been a realtor in this market, the slow conditions of the market would have amplified the challenges we were facing on the cash-flow side because we wouldn't have been generating income from deals either.

Regardless of how you do it, if you want to become a full time real estate investor, you'll need to find a cash-today strategy that works for you so you don't have to wait 10 years before you can call it quits. Basically, that means you're going to have to create a job for yourself ... so it's really your choice whether you do something in real estate or you find cash elsewhere. As I said before, some days a job at Starbucks looks pretty darn nice!

HOW DO YOU KNOW WHAT STRATEGY IS RIGHT FOR YOU?

What is holding you back from creating the life you love? It's not complicated. *The only thing holding you back is YOU.*

The single biggest character trait that is evident in successful real estate investors is simply *the willingness to take action.* In the face of fear, successful investors just take a step. After a big screw up, successful investors get up and keep moving. A successful deal doesn't stop successful investors either; they keep making things happen. They learn from what works and what doesn't.

Success is elusive to those who sit on their ass.

The missing piece is always action.

If you are ready to take action and keep taking action, then you will succeed. Period.

I'm about to lay out the foundation of successful real estate investing, but before we get to more specifics of what to do, I want to reveal the secret that completely changed how we approach our investments. I also believe it's the secret that is going to help you figure out if you need to pick a cash-today strategy that includes real estate or not! Because what I find is that most of us reach a point where real estate seems like the only choice that will make us money and that is simply not true.

THE SECRET

Your entire life as an investor gets easier when you take the time to figure out why you are investing in real estate. What do you want an average day in your life to look like?

DON'T YOU DARE FLIP PAST THIS SECTION!
THIS IS SO IMPORTANT!

It's a wild ride ... and if you're investing in real estate, you're going to want the secret that gets you through the tough stuff and out the other side – so you can *enjoy* the massive benefits of being a real estate investor.

In the moments when it all feels so overwhelming – whether you're cleaning up a bathroom that four young guys used for a year without ever cleaning; or you're looking for the seventh lender in the hopes of funding your deal; or you're digging deep trying to find your first deal – *take a step back and remember why you wanted to invest in real estate in the first place.*

WHAT MAKES YOU WANT TO BECOME A REAL ESTATE INVESTOR?

Many investors say the answer is financial freedom. Others may say passive income. But these answers aren't good enough to keep you going through the tough stuff that you *will* encounter. Hopefully I've already convinced you of the meaninglessness of those words. And if I haven't, let me put it to you this way:

If you got into real estate to make $5,000 a month in passive income or to buy 50 properties, you might get there but you're probably not going to be happy.

Real estate investing success is not about getting to some number. If that's what you're chasing, it's going to be very hard work; and when you hit the really big obstacles, you'll give up or make yourself miserable.

It's not enough to pursue financial freedom or passive income. There needs to be a much bigger reason. *There must be a clear vision. And that vision has to go beyond money.*

When your tenant pulls a knife on her roommate, and then stops paying rent when the roommate moves out, and it takes you three months to evict the knife yielding tenant; money is not enough to keep going. When you discover that the roof you spent $10,000 repairing the year before is still leaking and requires another $7,000 to fix; and at the same time you discover a tree growing from the inside of the house out the window; giving up on real estate will be top of mind – right behind how the heck am I going to pay for all of this? (Yes – all those things happened to us.)

So you need to ask yourself: Why do I want to invest in real estate?

If the answer is for financial freedom or passive income, then the next question to ask yourself is:

Why do you want financial freedom / passive income?

Because I want to be able to leave my job and live my life the way I want.

Why?

Because I want to spend more time with my family and because I believe I have a bigger purpose in life than working for someone else all my life.

Why?

If you keep going down this path you'll eventually end up in a place that lets you know that you are pursuing all of these things for the simple reason that you think they will make you feel happy and fulfilled.

We used to believe we were passionate about real estate.

We like doing deals. Dave loves running the numbers. I like looking at properties and finding the deals. I like thinking strategically about the risks and how we can make money.

That's not passion though. I think that's excitement. I'm excited about what real estate offers. It offers financial comfort and security; and that comfort and security allows us to dedicate more time to helping other investors avoid mistakes and create a life they love, thanks to rental property.

Making money is exciting. I like it a lot. I like that real estate is a fantastic way to make money over time. I'm not passionate about real estate though, and here's how I know:

If I was told I could never do another real estate deal in my life, I wouldn't be devastated. In some ways, if I'm honest with myself, I would feel a bit of relief. It's so much work to continuously do deals, and being forced to take a break from it would be nice.

On the other hand, if you told me I wasn't allowed to teach others anything for the rest of my life, I would be lost. I would have no purpose in my life.

You have to dig deep. If you want to be a real estate investor for money, it's not going to be enough to get you through the low times.

A good friend of mine started down the road of becoming a real estate investor. He had the big goal of buying 50 properties. There's nothing wrong with that. The problem was he was really seeking fulfillment in his life.

Today you would never know he's the same guy that was chasing all those properties. He's writing books, loving time with his family, and they're choosing where they live and what they spend time on – and he didn't get there through real estate. Real estate is not the only possible solution – it just might be the only one you've considered so far.

When you realize that, and when you understand that it's not that quick, and it's definitely not that easy, you may find that real estate is not at all the place to start.

Or you may find, as we have, that real estate is an effective vehicle to help you take a big step towards the big WHY's in your life.

Don't get me wrong … we all need money. But once your basic needs are taken care of, you need a lot more than money to feel happy. You need to figure out the WHY in your life.

Who is setting your goals?

We always ask our potential coaching clients to complete an application form. Working with people who are the right fit for what we offer is important to us. We only coach a small number of people each year, so we want to work with people that we can help in a massive way.

When we first started asking people to complete the forms, I was absolutely baffled by the numbers people had set for themselves as goals. We would ask questions like: What do you want to accomplish in the next 12 months? We had so many people responding that they wanted to buy eight properties or 17 in the next year. Those numbers were *so* strange. How did people come up with them? And why did so many people think eight or 17 was the magic number for the next year?

Eventually I realized it was because they were looking to

earn recognition from a club they belonged to, and those were the levels at which you could earn recognition.

I loved that these folks were keen to take action, and that looking forward to earning a reward had them excited about making things happen, but my concern was that *someone else had given them a goal.* Even more concerning was that the goal was based on the number of properties and nothing else. "Seventeen properties" is not such a good thing if it doesn't move you closer to living the life you want to live. And it's definitely not a good thing if you're buying *any* property just to get your recognition and reward.

In 2005, we woke up to the realization that the dozen properties we owned had taken us in exactly the opposite direction to what we actually wanted to create in our lives. We had set out in pursuit of wealth, yes; but more specifically we wanted to make enough money so that we had control over our time.

Instead of creating freedom, we had effectively created total chaos, stress and financial strain in our lives. We owned properties in four different cities at that time, worked with four different property managers, and were experiencing serious problems that ranged from bad tenants to fire code violations to shady property managers.

Yes, for a while we were actually making really good money. In fact, most of the properties we've owned have had positive cash flow. One of our properties produced $1200/month positive cash flow.

For us, it wasn't that we had tried to squeeze ourselves with deals where the numbers didn't work (which is a very common problem with investors who are pursuing a certain number of deals). Our problem was that we were too spread out and not involved enough with our properties. How can you be involved when your properties are all over Canada?

We realized we weren't clear on why we were investing. We were pursuing no-money-down deals and riches. We'd allowed a real estate course to tell us the deals we should do, and we ended up with a giant mess of a portfolio that took years to clean up. We made decisions based on where we thought the most money was to be made and we ended up very unhappy.

Owning properties in different cities sounds sexy but the reality is: it's chaotic. You can't rely on your local team to solve problems because your rock star plumber in Nanaimo, BC can't help you in Niagara Falls, Ontario. And your fabulous handyman in Toronto isn't going to commute to Niagara Falls to fix your units.

Five properties that are paid off will do a lot more for you than 17 that are leveraged as much as possible. Three great deals will do more for you than eight bad ones.

Numbers aren't the most important consideration as a real estate investor – despite what most investors will tell you. *What's important is whether each deal you do moves you closer or further away from the life you want to live.* Make sure you're setting goals for yourself, based on what you are trying to create for you and your family.

When we got clear on what we wanted real estate to do for us, and what we wanted our typical day to look like, we sold all our Ontario properties, and kept only our properties in BC. We eventually moved to Nanaimo, where 80% of our holdings are, and we focused on building a team to help us. Now everything is much simpler and we continue to look for ways to make things even simpler.

We didn't get into real estate to complicate things, but that is exactly what we did until we got clear on why we wanted to be in real estate.

WHERE TO INVEST

All right – you're still with me, so that's a good sign.

I don't want you getting into real estate lightly – without thinking carefully about what you're doing.

I see a lot of people who get into real estate and definitely aren't ready for what's about to hit them. Some retreat with their tail between their legs; others become bitter and tired – resenting their property and their tenants. And many others rush off to find an easier way. They think they *must* be doing something wrong to make it so hard – so they take some of the big-promises, get-rich-quick type courses.

And the biggest thing I hear from all of them is that *they had no idea it could be such a rough ride.* (As a side note, the ones who pick themselves up and try again are almost always very successful!)

WHAT NOBODY ELSE WILL TELL YOU ABOUT HOW TO SUCCESSFULLY INVEST IN REAL ESTATE

Everything we've covered so far has been important for your foundation. A firm stance in reality, understanding why you want to invest in real estate, and being clear on what it can and can't do are critical to helping you reduce much of the pain and suffering we (and many other well intentioned investors) experienced when starting out.

However, the best foundation in the world doesn't help you if you aren't clear on the next steps. And, unfortunately, even some of the best training programs in North America still don't tell you ALL the things you need to know about each step. Some of them will actually send you down the wrong path if you aren't carefully considering whether their advice is what *you* need to achieve your life goals.

I see it all the time. We meet investors with property that makes very little sense, considering what they set out to achieve; but it's what they learned to do from the club they joined or training program they signed up for. Now they are unhappy with real estate or feeling stressed and uncertain. They think they need time management help or a kick in the butt … but what they really need is a whole new plan!

I want to explain what you need to do to create a simple, less risky, and probably more profitable real estate business than any other plan you'll find in Canada (and probably the U.S. too).

Of course our way is not the only way; but if you're trying to build wealth and still enjoy your life, take careful note of what we say versus what you'll commonly hear, read & learn from others.

First, ditch the idea that you have to find a perfect investment market. It doesn't exist. It's not in Edmonton. It's not in Phoenix. And it's certainly not in Nanaimo where we invest.

When I speak with people, some are actually ashamed of *where* they are investing because it's not on someone's Top 10 list. The ones who should be ashamed are the ones that awkwardly try to buy in Hamilton, Edmonton or some other market *just* because it's on a list. If you like to travel to Edmonton or Hamilton or Phoenix, and you're excited about the market and your team in that area, and you genuinely want to have distance between you and your investments – go for it.

I'm just suggesting that you be honest with yourself – would you be excited about investing in that market if someone else wasn't telling you that it's a hot place to invest?

As noted, most of our portfolio is in Nanaimo, BC. In all the years we've been buying in Nanaimo, it has *never* been on anybody's top-places-to-invest list. Some people who live there *can't believe* it's a good place to invest. Despite that, we've been consistently making good money in Nanaimo since 2001. Even when many investors suffered from the downturn in 2008, Nanaimo treated us well.

Every single market has positive and negative aspects. Some are better poised for capital appreciation. Others are more stable, i.e., you have to make your money on mortgage pay down and cash flow because you're not going to see values change much. And still, some markets are declining.

You can make money in all of these markets if you know what you're doing. So it's not necessarily about the market. It's more about matching your strategy with the market and the stage of the real estate cycle that market is in. And *most* importantly, it's about making sure you're buying property that fits with your WHY.

My preference is to invest in a market that is more stable – that's growing, but not rapidly; a market where nothing happens *too* quickly, allowing you time to make careful decisions. I like a market that doesn't generally shift overnight, so you don't run into massive increases or drops – both of which can cause you a lot of headaches as an investor. Most importantly though – I don't want to have to fly or drive too far to deal with my property issues.

One of our properties is literally behind my house. I can stand on my deck and look at all three units in the property. I can tell if the tenants are home. I know if they took their trash out. Their dog barks at my dogs and vice versa. If I have to handle something, it takes me 10 minutes, not two hours.

That's *my* preference. Yours might be different.

At one point, we owned property in six different cities across

Canada and we didn't live close to any of our investments. And we used to tell people that as if it were a good thing; like we were cool investors because we owned property in so many different places. We've come to realize, however, that it's *so much easier* to live close to where you invest. It's less hassle and easier to control what's happening. **When you have more control, you make more money with less effort.**

MY BOLD ASSUMPTION ABOUT YOU

You may say you are interested in becoming a "full-time real estate investor," but chances are that actually means you want freedom, minimal hassles and nobody bossing you around.

You don't actually want to be "full time."

Our client Ian Kennedy said it best when he stated: "I want a full-time income from real estate, but I'm not interested in full-time work from real estate."

In other words, when you buy property you aren't really looking to buy yourself a full-time job, are you?

The big fancy pants U.S. guru to whom we gave $20,000 didn't have any of his coaches and teachers explain that concept to us. We learned to look for properties with a GRM of 10 or less (if you don't know what a GRM is, that's okay; I will explain it shortly). We learned to find deals that cash-flowed buckets, had motivated sellers willing to do creative deals, and that we could buy with little to no money down.

We chased those juicy deals all over the place. We did deals in three different cities in less than a year. Then we had the glorious problem of managing problems in three different cities ... and *trust me* ... if you're finding deals with motivated sellers *and* massive cash flow, you're finding problem properties. If you have a property that can cash flow positively $1,500 per month, *why would you ever sell it unless it's challenging to manage?*

My assumption about *you* is that you want to enjoy your life. You want time to hang out with your family. You want the comfort of knowing that you are unlikely to find yourself dealing with a property manager who has been charged with manslaughter. You want to find great deals that will make you money, attract great tenants, and *not* fall apart on you after a few months.

If I am right about you, the next five chapters are going to help you in a BIG way.

I am going to lay out the exact steps we follow to find under-market deals in our market area; how we attract great tenants, often commanding higher than market rents; and how we make more money with less effort from our deals.

THE GREAT BUNNY CHASE

We have two awesome dogs. Bram and Maya. Bram, our older dog, loves to chase anything that will run away. We used to take him to a particular park that has hundreds of bunnies living there. The bunnies would be scattered everywhere. When we let Bram off his leash he would start chasing one, only to see two still asleep off to his left. He'd abandon the first bunny and go after the two sleeping ones. They'd wake up and run away. He'd then switch and go after one eating grass.

Happily for me, he never caught a bunny; all he ever did was wear himself out. His mistake, of course, was trying to chase all of them at once. If he had focused on one little bunny, he just might have had a chance, but he never did. Instead, he was always changing direction and thinking the next bunny HAD to be easier to catch.

Does this sound like your attempts at real estate investing? Or wealth creation in general? If so, you're definitely not alone.

As humans, we are easily distracted. By default, we are generally lazy, always looking for something more interesting than what is in front of us right now. In case you don't believe me, let me ask you: Have you ever been walking down the street – focused on getting somewhere in record time – only to stop dead in your tracks when you spot a penny or a dime and are tempted to stoop down to pick it up?

That's not the only way we allow low-value objects, goals, or priorities to distract us from more important things. We interrupt conversations with family members to comment on silly commercials on television. We check our iPhones in the middle of a workout. And we allow e-mail to interrupt higher priority activities on the job.

It's a good thing to consider your options, but don't let them distract you from what's been working for you and helping you achieve your goals.

If you have an investing strategy that is working for you – stick to it and master it.

Though there are plenty of ways to make money in real estate, the optimal route is to find a strategy you like and get really good at it. Stay focused and become a specialist in your investing niche and you, too, will find your wealth grow very quickly.

By the way – I don't take Bram to that park anymore. I am afraid one day he might figure out the secret and actually catch one.

THE FORMULA WE USE: BUYING PROPERTIES WITH A "CAUSE"

When someone comes to me complaining about the lack of cash-flowing deals, I ask where they've been looking. Usually I get a response like: "I spent nearly two hours on MLS last night searching the entire city, and I didn't see a single deal that would work." Then, for good measure, they often offer up some other market that they looked at online and it wasn't any better.

There are so many reasons this approach fails and the first one is lack of focus. The first thing you have to do is *choose your market*. From there, focus on finding great deals.

Here is *our formula* for only buying properties with a CAUSE.

CAUSE:
- Convenience
- Attracts families
- Under the average price
- Starter home
- Economic fundamentals.

Convenience: Is the property near schools, hospitals, shopping, public transportation, a university? The more convenient the location, generally the more in demand it will be, both for renting and for selling in the future. It also increases the potential rent rate and the quality of the rental pool you'll draw from.

Attracts families: Areas that attract families and that fit all the other CAUSE categories tend to be the easiest to rent – with less turnover, lower maintenance and lower risk.

Under the average price: We focus on buying homes that are 10% below the average price in our chosen market. Why only 10% below? Because if you go much below that, you tend to get into tougher neighbourhoods and rougher houses – and just because we buy in areas that are 10% below the average house price for our city doesn't mean the houses we buy are only 10% under – we're bargain hunting!

Starter home: Determine what type of home in your chosen city/market is a starter home (single family detached house, townhouse, or condominium) and then buy those types of homes. This is the entry level home and tends to be the most liquid, the most price stable, and generally the easiest to rent out. People move up from them and down into them.

Economic fundamentals: Find a city that you are near and that has good market fundamentals (people are moving there, more jobs are coming, amenities and infrastructure are growing, government is pro-business, rent rates are stable or increasing).

CHOOSING YOUR INVESTMENT MARKET

When you know what signs you are looking for in a market, you'll find it's fairly simple to pick a good location for your investing. It's not about finding the *perfect* market area because *that perfect area does not exist!*

I've seen investors race all over the country trying to find the *perfect* investment market. I've also seen people freeze up because it's *overwhelming* to try to pick the perfect market.

It's not about finding the perfect market – it's about finding a market with decent fundamentals that will also allow you to live the life you WANT to live.

When evaluating areas, we recommend you consider the following elements:

- Familiar area
- Population growth
- Good employment
- Good transportation
- Healthy housing economy
- Appealing opportunities.

For some of the above items you want to see *trends* and where they are heading over a longer period of time for the overall market – like population growth, for example. But, you will also want to find out what factors may *impact* that trend.

In other words, knowing that the population of Regina was

ranked #1 by Money Sense Magazine in their 2012 survey of Best Places To Live may get you pretty excited to invest there; more people means more renters which means more income, right? However, when you find out that the year before it was ranked 116 out of 180 surveyed cities, the questions you should be asking are:

What is driving the growth right now? (In other words, was it a one-time event or can I count on that kind of growth?) *Will that driver be sustainable?*

Of course, in a survey comparing cities like the Money Sense one (LINK: http://www.moneysense.ca/2012/03/20/ top-35-best-places-to-live-in-2012/05_regina/) so many other factors could be impacting the numbers to make Regina look better than it really is. For example, a smaller population base to begin with could make its growth on a percentage basis much larger than other cities getting a substantially greater growth in population in terms of number of people. The big thing is to not automatically rely on anybody's lists, rankings or suggestions of averages or trends. *Dig deeper to find out why* you are seeing the trend you are seeing and whether there is something skewing the average.

For all these reasons, I highly encourage you to begin investing in an area *you already know well.* It reduces your learning curve significantly, and unless the market you are in right now is shrinking (like Windsor, Ontario was a couple of years ago) or is very expensive (like Vancouver, BC), you will have an easier time starting if you focus close to home.

As you research all of the elements on the checklist, think about prospective tenants. Where will they work? How will they get to work? Where else would they live, if not in the area you are looking at? And, of course, think about an exit strategy. *Buy each property with the end in mind.* It doesn't matter if you plan to live in the property or rent it out ... before you buy, envision yourself selling it.

You are making an investment only if there is a reasonable probability that you will make money on it while you own it and that you will be able to make money when you sell. Good location research before you buy the property will increase the likelihood of making a lot of money from the property!

You are looking for areas that are growing or are about to grow. If the places you already know are shrinking, pick a place somewhere else that you can become familiar with (ideally somewhere that is within a reasonable driving distance). For me, a reasonable driving distance is under two hours. Your acceptable distance may be less or more. Just imagine that you have to go there twice in a week – what distance would you be okay driving twice in a week if it was important?).

As you are picking a place, think about your general sense of the area, and ask yourself:

1. Is the *population growing* or at least stable?
2. Is the *average income* (single and/or household) increasing faster than other areas?
3. Is the *population ageing or is it younger*? If the percentage is growing for seniors and shrinking for youth, it may not be a great place to invest; having an older population usually means the area is not growing and nor is the economy growing. But if it's a retirement destination, obviously a growing population of seniors is a good thing!
4. Is the area's *economy* growing? Is there new construction? Are companies adding jobs?
5. Are the number of *schools* increasing or decreasing in that area? Similar to point 3 above, if you have a younger population moving into the area, those are often good signs that you'll be able to rent your unit (because demand for housing will be high).
6. What's the general sense in the *media* about the area?

When you are getting the sense of an area, we have one BIG word of caution: don't just follow blogs and forums that are not linked in some way to a reputable company or the government. You want to get accurate information, not what "John the realtor says about Calgary, Alberta." It doesn't hurt to get some information from sites like that, but stick to the facts! Someone who makes money when *you* do a deal may not be presenting the full picture of what is happening. You want all the data so you can make your own informed decision.

Starting with an area you already know reduces your learning curve when you are starting out. It's tempting to just dive right in at the first positive sign anywhere, *but it is imperative that you really familiarize yourself with an area before you invest in property there.* If you don't, you might luck out and invest in a good area, or you might find yourself struggling to find tenants and quickly losing money.

Okay, how do you do your research to ensure you've found a growing area? *Your best source of information on population and income growth is your local government.* And thanks to the internet, you may not even have to do much work to get the information you need.

Here are a few other places to start with ... but if you don't get very far, don't be shy about picking up the phone and calling the local government of the area you're interested in and asking questions about the trends....

CANADIAN RESOURCES:

- http://www.cmhc-schl.gc.ca/ (they have great City Profiles)
- http://www.statcan.gc.ca

US RESOURCES:

- http://www.census.gov/population/www/index.html
- http://www.census.gov/population/www/pop-profile/profile.html

Your best bet is to go to google.com and type in "population growth your city" or some variation of that. You will likely find all sorts of interesting stats and figures about your chosen market. It takes a while to sift through the information; but once you've found some good sites with useful information, bookmark them on your computer or write the website address down and keep it in an easy-to-find place for future reference!

A new Canadian population census just came out in 2012, so for Canada, most data is relatively up-to-date.

WHAT YOU ARE LOOKING TO LEARN:

The trends. Over a five to ten-year timeframe (or longer), have more people been consistently moving into the area than moving out?

Where the new people are coming from. Are they from other places within the province or state, or from a different part of the country? Or, are they from a different country? A good mix of people coming from all over is the healthiest sign. Growth coming from one place only is always a concern because something could change and reverse that growth quickly.

How do these trends and the information you've learned compare to other cities. Is this area stronger and more diverse in its growth than most of the cities in the country? What about in that province or state?

What is the reason for the growth? You will investigate this further when you look into employment, but a sense of whether they are coming in to work in the Oil Sands or coming in to work at the new local Google office is important. Workers who arrive for a one-year contract are good renters in the short run, but who will you be renting to when they leave? Lately, there has been a lot of excitement on the East Coast with the ship building contract that was secured in Halifax, and the growth in the Maritime provinces in the coming years, thanks to that contract, will be significant. But will the growth in the areas you choose to invest in continue over the long term? This is what you need to understand. If workers are only going to move in while they have work and then move back to where they came from when the work is over, you'll want to have a shorter term strategy in mind if you still decide to invest in that market.

When a local Wendy's fast food restaurant is paying $18/hr for part-time work, many people believe there is nothing but money to be made. This has happened in the past up in Grande Prairie and other Northern Alberta locations; and people from all over the world rushed into the great north in search of riches. But this type of rapid growth is not sustainable ... and many of the landlords up there got burned. Too many people were trying to squeeze into properties. The stories of 10 people sharing a 1-bedroom unit are legendary. Imagine the wear and tear on your place! Sure, you're making a more-than-decent rental rate, but at what cost? *In short, keep in mind that you're not looking for a crazy spike in growth; you're looking for a stable trend moving in a positive direction.*

Most cities have websites that will tell you about their major industries and employers. Once you know the major companies in a market, learn more about them. Search the local papers for any news about each company. You can also go into the City Offices and speak to someone in the city development office. You can let them know that you're looking at doing some real estate investing in the area, and you'd like to speak to someone whose job it is to attract and work with new businesses in the area.

Note: If no such person exists, that is a problem in itself! There should be someone who handles economic development in the city.

Researching population growth will also naturally lead you into learning about the employment situation in the area. For jobs and income details, you're really just trying to see if your market is healthy or coming down with a cold.

People making money – and, in particular, people making more money than in other areas – is a great indicator of an area's good health. A market with low levels of unemployment will usually be a very healthy place to invest in real estate. Good employment opportunities attract workers from other areas and will usually offer competitive wages in order to fill those jobs with skilled and qualified workers. Your pool of renters will be full of people that are employed – with stable incomes that can be used to pay *you* each month.

Your research sources for employment can also be the sources you used to find out about population growth, but expanding your research to include more sources will help a lot.

Questions you need answers for include:
What is the current unemployment rate in the market?

- Is this number going up or going down?
- Who are the major employers in the market? Are they expanding or contracting?
- Are there any new companies entering the market?
- Is the government doing anything that will create new jobs? (Infrastructure improvements like those that happened in Vancouver for the 2010 Olympics involved a major investment from the government and created many thousands of new jobs.)

You will have a very good sense of the area's economic health after researching the employment and population changes in the area. You should now know about the job trends and even the income trends. Is the average income increasing at a faster rate than the rest of the city, province, state or country? What about job creation in that area? What are the plans for new jobs or expansion of companies or city boundaries?

The final thing you *really* have to evaluate is *the health of the housing market*. Even a strong growing population and good jobs is not enough to keep up with excessive building or a ton of housing inventory, so you have to look at what's available as well as what is coming up.

The health of the housing market is impacted by all of the things you've been researching up to this point, *and* by what is happening with prices, rent rates and inventory, so take a look at the trends around…:

- Sales to listing ratios
- Rental rate trends
- House price trends
- Vacancy rates.

Again, dig deeper and ask yourself *why* things are up or down.

FIGURING OUT RENT RATES

Figuring out rent rates for your area and what is happening with the rental market is *always* going to be a critical skill as an investor – not just when you're *finding* deals but also while you're holding them! So, let's pause here and spend a bit of time discussing this important piece of the puzzle.

Questions you want to try and answer when you are researching rental rate trends include:

- The specific rent rates for different bedroom sizes. What is the average two-bedroom unit renting for in my area? Check one-bedroom units as well.
- What is the average rental rate for the area? What was that rate last year? What about 6 months ago? Is it more, less or the same?

- What government controls exist on rents? Some areas have rent control, and that poses artificial controls on the market rents; so when you're evaluating the numbers, you'll want to know if that is the case.

WHERE TO LOOK (FOR CANADIANS):

- Rentometer (http://www.rentometer.com/)
- Craigslist (http://www.craigslist.org/)
- Kijiji (http://www.kijiji.com/)
- Local newspapers
- Search for landlord/tenant legislation for your area to find out about rent controls.
- CMHC (http://www.cmhc-schl.gc.ca/).

WHERE TO LOOK (FOR AMERICANS):

- Rent.com
- Craigslist (http://www.craigslist.org/)
- Local newspapers
- Search for landlord/tenant legislation for your area to find out about rent controls – many states do have very strict landlord legislation to be aware of.
- http://www.letstalkpm.com/ a great resource to find just about anything you need to know about rentals in the U.S.
- Bigger Pockets Forums (http://www.biggerpockets.com/).

We also drive around our chosen area, and we also call the numbers on the FOR RENT signs that are not those of professional property managers (you know – the homemade ones or the signs bought at Staples). We like to get a sense of what's available, what they are asking, and what amenities or features they emphasize (if any). We don't need to call the professionally managed properties because a quick look on their website usually provides us with all the details we need.

Also, take a look at housing starts and how many of them are condos, apartments, or other properties that may impact the current rent stock and rental rates.

In 2009, we bought a couple of properties in Kelowna, BC. Prices were down and we saw a few opportunities to buy in fabulous areas with growth potential. The single-family home we purchased as a rent to own did fabulously and we sold it to the tenants a year later. The two-suited home near the lake, however, has been a struggle for us ever since. While it's in a stellar location and in good condition, the challenge has been the large number of condos that have been built in Kelowna. Because they didn't sell, the builders rented them out, dramatically increasing the rental stock in the area.

It's economics 101 to know that when supply goes up without an increase in demand, it puts downward pressure on rents. Our rents dropped several hundred dollars a unit – *killing* our cash flow. We've been feeding the property a few thousand dollars every year since we bought it.

The market in Kelowna continues to be strong with a positive future, but the short term holding of rental units in that area is painful. We grossly underestimated how many units were still to come on the market, how many were still vacant at the time, and how much pressure that would put on rents over the next few years.

WATCH OUT FOR OTHER POTENTIAL CHALLENGES AND OPPORTUNITIES

Keep your eyes and ears open as you do your research. There are many other things that can impact real estate in a local market. You are looking out for factors that could have a negative impact as well as factors that will flag this area as one set to grow and prosper.

How to spot the other opportunities (or dangers)? Look out for:

Government Plans: We've already mentioned the government,

but the role they play in real estate investing cannot be emphasized enough. New rules and regulations can create or kill opportunities. In Ontario and BC, Canada, the introduction of the HST tax in the summer of 2010 created a lull in the market that created opportunities for savvy investors watching out for that opportunity. Another example: a ban on development in one area will impact other areas where development can take place – the Green Belt in Toronto, for instance, caused some major changes in housing development and opportunities. It's difficult to say exactly what you have to watch out for, but read the local news and get a handle on what the local government is doing, as well as any legislative changes in the works that will impact you as a property owner. Other ideas to watch out for: for U.S. investors, changes to the REO/Foreclosure process; for investors everywhere, the changes to how real estate agents can offer their services will play a role in the market, as well as tax changes, zoning changes, etc.

Interest Rates: What people *think* is going to happen with interest rates will trigger a short term opportunity. It is not going to drive the overall economy for a long period of time unless it also becomes the case that financing becomes either readily available or not easily available. Having an understanding of what interest rates are doing and how they impact investments in your area is important. I highly recommend that you pick up a book or two by Kieran Trass so you can start getting a good understanding of interest rates and their impact on housing and the real estate cycle. The important thing with interest rates is to watch overall housing affordability and the *perception* of what is happening to interest rates – not so much what the interest rate actually *is* at the time. For Canadians, there is a new book out by Greg Head, Christine Ruptash, Don R. Campbell, and Kieran Trass entitled *Secrets of the Canadian Real Estate Cycle* and it's an excellent resource for understanding real estate cycles.

New Development: When we bought a condo in North York, Ontario in 2001, we were burned by buying in an area that was about to explode. A little research would have told us that the area was soon to be flooded with units similar to what we were buying. Ten years later, that condo would have been a fabulous investment because all that stock has now been absorbed, but five years later when we had to sell it, we found ourselves competing with brand new units that were not much more money. Needless to say, we didn't make money on that sale. An area that has been flooded, but that has good indicators otherwise, could be a good opportunity if you are able to hold on for the long term and attract good tenants in the meantime. On the other hand, if there is something preventing new development in an area, that is actually a positive thing in most cases. It often means existing properties will go up in value. But it can also mean that area will just die off and lose out to the newer, more interesting areas being developed. Learning about the area will give you a good indication of what is happening. If businesses and governments are investing in that area despite a lack of new development, it's a very good sign.

Availability of Land: This is very much related to new development, but it is important to look at as you drive around a potential area to spot opportunities. If there's plenty of land and empty lots around and there are no limits on development, it's likely that supply will continue to grow to meet demand. And keep in mind that a small parcel of land can turn into a multi-unit complex that will house dozens of families; so just because there are only one or two good pieces of land in an area doesn't mean there won't be any large developments. But it's still a factor to consider.

CHAPTER FIVE

HOW TO CREATE DEALS THAT MAKE MONEY

It is really hard work to find great deals that will cash flow consistently; but not many people in the real estate industry are going to tell you that. If they told you how hard it was going to be, you wouldn't want to buy their system or hire them to be your real estate agent. They will make it sound easy so you get excited and want their help. There's no way around it, though. If you want to do great deals you have a lot of work ahead of you.

It happens almost every time I speak – especially at real estate events on the West Coast of Canada. I get on stage and talk about some of our recent deals and the money each property brings in every month, and then after my talk I am almost attacked by frustrated investors…. "I spend hours on MLS and I never see anything that works" is the most common comment people make after they hear that many of our properties are generating positive cash flow of $400 - $800 per month. We have some that bring in a little less, and a couple that bring in a lot more, but most of our properties are within that range, and all of them are in British Columbia.

The trick to finding great cash flowing deals in any market isn't about knowing how to run numbers on houses you find on MLS. You *can* find great deals on MLS – we do about half our deals straight from MLS – but there is a lot more to it than just looking online.

Most great deals are not found – they are *created*. You need to know how to *create* deals through adding value, negotiating, solving problems and spotting opportunities. The easiest way to be able to do this is to *become an area expert* and mine that area for opportunities.

Once you have your market selected, you then choose one or two *submarkets* within that city. You're looking for *pockets with potential*. Inside that pocket, you want a starving crowd of renters looking for good quality homes, and you want to get to know exactly what they are looking for.

Ideally, you also want to be in an area where first-time home buyers like to buy. That will help you out with your exit strategy when you want to sell in the future (or, if you're doing rent to own, it will ensure you have a healthy market of potential tenant buyers to select from).

A submarket is a small area. You can walk around it in about 40 minutes. We owned a triplex in Toronto that was in a perfect example of a sub-market. This sub-market, in our view, was the area between Bathurst and Ossington and from Bloor Street to College Street. That's roughly 22 blocks –11 across and 2 long blocks down.

When you go across any major streets like those ones named above, the quality and type of homes change, or the area changes from residential to other property uses.

Your sub-market should have home prices below the city average, but rents similar to other, higher priced areas.

That's the part a lot of our coaching clients miss the first time they start trying to select a sub-market area to focus on. The key to making this work in your area is to look at the average price of the *type* of property you're going to buy (i.e., don't just look at the average price of a home if you're focusing on condos – look at the average price of a condo).

When you know that number, you can begin focusing on areas in your city where that price is lower – not dramatically lower because that usually means it's a bad area – but lower. Then you look at rent rates for the type of property you're going to target (we target 3 or 4-bedroom single family homes with a minimum of 2 bathrooms). You are then looking for an area where the rent rate is basically the same as in a higher-end area but the house prices are lower.

Our primary target area in Nanaimo has an average house price of about $350,000. That house will rent out for about $1,700. (Now, hold your horses a minute; that is not the deal we do ... that's just the numbers we're working with to identify the pocket of potential to focus on.) A comparable area further north in the city will have similar houses for $420,000 – $450,000 and the rent is no more than $1,800 for those houses.

In other words, we can buy a house for $100,000 less and basically get the same rent rates. Those are the kind of numbers we're looking for – and after coaching a few hundred people across Canada, I can assure you that most markets have areas like this.

The chosen sub-market also needs to be strong in accessibility, quality of schools, and local jobs. Good areas to start looking are around major transportation hubs (sky trains, subways, bus stops, major roads), major facilities like a hospital or a university, or even major government buildings, shopping, etc.

With your market area selected, your big job now is to stay focused on your property type in that submarket. If you're going to buy townhomes, focus on townhomes. Don't get distracted by every property type in your submarket, at least not at first. You can always add a type or a market later, once you're an expert on the first one. You're not stuck with this for life, but you have to become an expert on the area and one property type before you can move on to another.

CONDOMINIUMS

Condominiums (condos) are becoming more and more common in urban areas as the price of land rises and the sheer cost of living close to the center of any city becomes prohibitive for the average person. The concept of a condo, whether in Canada or the United States, is that you have ownership of your unit and shared ownership of the land and other parts of the building. In fact, "condominium" or "condo" is actually a legal term, although in British Columbia (where we live) they are also referred to as strata properties, and in Quebec they are called co-proprietorships.

Many people think of a high rise building when they hear the word "condominium," but in reality a detached home can be a condominium just as easily as a unit in a high rise building. It simply means the land that the detached home sits on is a common element.

This means that the unit is owned by the person (or company) on title, but that everyone shares the cost and ownership for common elements such as walkways, driveways, hallways, lobbies, security, amenities like workout rooms and pools, stairways, electrical systems and other things that are not part of the space that belongs to individual owners.

As an investor, you need to be aware of the maintenance fees that are associated with a condo property.

In properties where costs have been poorly managed or where there have been a lot of problems, the maintenance fees can be very high. Make sure you factor the monthly maintenance fees into your analysis of the property; forgetting them will really eat into your cash flow. What's more, these fees will not remain the same year over year – they will often go up and up and up! We've *never* seen maintenance fees drop ... and you will not have any choice but to pay the increasing fees.

The maintenance fees on a condo typically include security, general maintenance and repair of the common elements, operating costs (trash and recycling, snow removal, yard care), as well as the accumulation of a contingency fund which will be used to cover the costs of any expenses that are not in the operating budget. Usually these will be the larger items; for example, roof replacement or parking lot repairs. If you do buy a condo, make sure you review the strata or condo minutes from past meetings to get a sense of how the building is being managed and any potential issues that may require a special one-time fee charge. We had two $600 fees laid on us in one year when we owned our townhome in Burnaby because our parking garage kept getting broken into. Something had to be done to prevent thieves from getting in, but that hadn't been planned for in the budget. This is just a minor example of what can be levied on you; but if this were an investment property, that $1200 probably would have eaten away four months of positive cash flow!

SINGLE FAMILY HOMES

Single family homes are probably the simplest investment to pursue. Most people have lived in a house, so they can relate to the decisions involved in home selection. It's typically easier to find tenants for a single family home and it's typically easier to attract a lender to finance the property. Also, single family homes generally hold their value much better than the other options in the residential market.

With single family homes, keep in mind that somebody needs to be responsible for the upkeep of the yard and snow removal. We try to include this in the rental agreements with tenants; but remember: it's still *your* responsibility to ensure it gets done.

The challenge with single family homes is that *most* areas in North America where you want to invest do not have many homes that will cash flow *without a second unit*. With only one unit in a home, it's very challenging to buy the home and have the rent cover the mortgage, maintenance and property management *and* still put cash in your pocket. To make purchases like this work, we generally work hard *to buy under the market value and then add a legal suite or put it into our rent to own program.*

CASE STUDY: FROM $10,000 TO $118,000 IN 6 YEARS
Do you really know what's possible?

If you say "yes," then my next question for you is: have you actually allowed yourself to set goals based on what is possible?

If you're like my husband Dave and myself, you likely haven't.

One of the downfalls of goal setting is that everyone tells you that a goal has to be realistic. This is true to a degree.

But realistic goal-setting doesn't mean you have to know how you will do something.

In other words, most of us edit our goals based on what we know how to do right now – or what we're capable of right now.

That's not what's possible. What is possible is usually way cooler, way more fun and way more lucrative.

Sometimes, all it takes to open your mind to what is possible is someone sharing something they did and how it worked for them.

That's what I want to do for you. I want to open up some possibilities for you by sharing a case study of one of our investment properties. It's not even close to our best deal, and it barely had positive cash flow (around $100/month) for five of the six years we owned it…. But I want to share it with you for two reasons:

One, I want you to see that real estate investing is a powerful way to make money in several different ways. Even if one way is not strong or not present at all, you are still likely to make money on an average deal.

Two, I want you to see what can happen when you open your door to *possibility* and try something a little different.

This is the story of a mediocre deal in a medium-paced housing market, and how we exited with an exceptional return on our investment.

We bought this Nanaimo, BC property in September 2005 and sold it in June 2011. We bought it in a hot market and sold it in a soft market.

By drawing on some equity in another property and getting bank financing, we were able to buy this property with only $10,000 out of our pocket.

From 2005 to 2010, it basically broke even each year. For most of those years, we didn't worry about the fact that it wasn't a super-duper cash-flowing property because we both had jobs.

When I left my job in 2008 and Dave had moved into the 100% commission business of commercial mortgage brokering (at a time when the banks practically stopped loaning to anyone!), we couldn't afford to have any of our properties underperforming. We needed cash coming in to pay our bills.

We began to reorganize our portfolio to create more cash flow, but we ignored this property initially because it had a good property manager, it had been headache free, and it wasn't costing us anything on a monthly basis.

As we rolled into 2009, we started to wonder about our property manager. Other properties he managed for us were suffering from neglect and we started to experience vacancies in this property as well as other properties – vacancies that had not been an issue previously.

Suddenly we had to pay attention. We had to spend money fixing up this particular property, and we were losing money because of vacancies – money we needed to live on. And we were not sure how to handle the issues with the property manager.

We actually listed the property for sale in 2009 but it didn't sell; we had very few showings and we didn't get a single offer.

Stuck with a property that was starting to cost us money, wasn't selling, and didn't have great management, we decided the best solution was to fix it up a bit more and try to turn it into a rent to own. We'd already done rent to own with property in

Kelowna and thought it might work in Nanaimo as well, but we weren't sure.

Unexpectedly we discovered a tremendous demand for rent to own in that area. The property filled instantly, and because it was now a rent to own, we:

- Received a $10,000 option fee which paid for all the upgrades and repairs we had to do.
- No longer had a property management expense because the tenant handled most maintenance issues.
- Received slightly higher rent because some of the rent went towards a credit they would receive when they bought.
- Created an exit strategy for the property that didn't require a realtor and made it easier to sell an investment property in a soft market.

Thirteen months later, the tenant successfully closed on the property and he is now a happy home owner. In the end, this mediocre property made us $118,000 and only required $10,000 out of our pocket in the six years we owned it.

The best part is that even if the property had not gone up in value, we still would have made a pretty awesome return on it. Here's how it looked:

Our Purchase Price:	$274,000
Our Sale Price:	$344,000
Appreciation:	$70,000
Mortgage Pay Down:	$33,000
Cash Flow:	$15,000
Total Cash Return over 6 years:	$118,000

Most of the $15,000 in cash flow was from the time that it was a rent to own property. It was generating a lot of cash flow for us as a rent to own because we increased the rent and dropped our property manager. Plus we filled the vacancy on our own – saving us the placement fee we were paying the PM.

Let's look at the return. We put in $10,000, so here's how the non-compounded return numbers looked:

	Total	Average Annual
Appreciation	700%	117%
Mortgage Pay Down	330%	55%
Cash Flow	150%	25%
Total Return	1,180%	197%

The point of this is to show you three things:

1. There are a lot of ways to make money from real estate. Even if there had been *no* appreciation, we would still have made a *very* good return, thanks to the mortgage pay down and the cash flow. Our return would have crushed any mutual fund's performance with 80% annually ($48,000 on our $10,000 investment over the 6 years).
2. If we had sold through a realtor (assuming $16,000 realtor commission) and not turned it into a rent to own, our annual return would have been 153%. We took a property that we couldn't sell and that wasn't making us money on a monthly basis, and we turned it into a cash flow machine for 13 months *and* created an exit strategy that allowed us to exit without a realtor and for the best possible price at the time.
3. We were able to use less of our own cash to magnify the return – and we did this by refinancing one of our other investment properties. But we also could have used a line of credit or private money, or else partnered with an investor with capital to keep our ROI high.

Even cooler than the money we made, was that we helped a young guy who was struggling to qualify for bank financing to become a home owner. Without this program, he would still be a few years away from home ownership rather than a proud home owner.

The bottom line is that there are a lot of ways to make money from a rental property. A good understanding of what is *possible* can really change your perspective. Plus it's nice to see that even a mediocre deal in an average Canadian market can make really solid money in times like these.

Forget about the things you *think* are holding you back. Instead, *think about what's possible.*

DUPLEXES, TRIPLEXES, FOURPLEXES

Duplexes, triplex and fourplexes are often appealing to investors because they generate more income than a single family home and usually can be purchased for similar price points as homes. Our first investment property was a duplex, and we've also owned everything from triplexes to sixplexes. They do generate more income each month and they generally have a bit more positive cash flow, but there are a few significant disadvantages to these properties.

The two biggest disadvantages are that you have limited exit options and that it's going to be more work to manage the property while you own it. When it's time to exit and sell the property, your potential buyers are limited to investors. If your housing market is slow when you need to sell, you will have a very tiny pool of people who will be interested in buying your property. Offloading a fourplex in a slow market is difficult. And it's more work while you own it because you generally get a lower quality of tenant (although if you have a very high quality multi-unit property in a great area, this will not be the case). And if you plan to manage the property yourself, you will need to dedicate a lot more time to the property than you would if it were a single family property.

Dave wrote a great overview of multiplexes versus single family homes for our website revnyou.com. Here's his article:

Article By Dave Peniuk

THE BIG QUESTION: ARE SINGLE FAMILY HOMES OR MULTI-FAMILY HOMES A BETTER INVESTMENT?

Many of our readers, and also yours truly, are constantly asking which is the better buy for an investor: a **single family home** (aka SFH) or a **multi-family home** (aka MFH)? Well, I am writing this to *finally* put an end to the debate!

For the purposes of this article, we'll consider either investment (SFH or MFH) to be a standard long-term buy and hold rental property (that means, not a reno, not a flip, not a lease to own, and not wholesaling, short-selling, day-trading or any other real estate strategy out there!).

Typically this type of discussion will take you down the road of buying Apartment Buildings versus Single Family Homes ... but I am going to do it a little differently. I am going to stick with where my experience has been – which is owning rental properties varying in size from one unit to six units.

So for the purposes of this article, a *SFH is defined* as a property (detached house, condo, townhouse, row house, etc.) that has only one unit and thus only one family living in it; *and a MFH, is defined* as any property that has more than one unit/family living in it. Thus, it could be a house with a basement suite (2 units), a duplex (2 units), a triplex (3 units), up to a sixplex (6 units).

ADVANTAGES OF INVESTING IN SINGLE FAMILY HOMES

- Depending on the city/area, they typically appreciate faster than MFHs.
- Generally a broader range of potential buyers (when it's time to sell).
- Often worth more on a per unit basis (but this can be a disadvantage too, as you pay more for it).
- More liquid – SFHs can often sell quicker, even in a down market, again due to a broader range of potential buyers.
- Only have to "deal" with one tenant, not many.
- Tenants don't argue with other tenants because they are the only ones living there! There will be no issues around

which tenant gets to use the barbecue or front patio, or even who puts out the garbage.

- Easier to get the tenants to pay for all of the utility bills, again because they are the only ones using them.
- Some argue that you get a better "quality" of tenant in a SFH than in a multi-family unit; however, I do not necessarily agree with this. I'll discuss why later.
- Financing your investment property is often simpler and easier to get.

DISADVANTAGES OF INVESTING IN SINGLE FAMILY HOMES

- The biggest disadvantage as an investor is that they rarely cash flow as well as a MFH.
- Can be "riskier" as there is only one tenant to pay the rent. If they vacate (and you can't immediately place a new tenant), who pays the mortgage, bills, utilities, etc.? *You* do! The MFH has more than 1 tenant, so at least you continue to collect *some* rent to offset your costs.
- SFHs tend to have a smaller pool of renters because SFHs tend to have higher rents than homes with multi-units. Thus, it may be more difficult to place a good tenant in a SFH.
- No economies of scale with a SFH. Most property managers (PMs) will offer discounts on a per unit basis if it's a MFH. The same goes for doing repairs and maintenance; you may get a cheaper per unit rate if you are replacing all the windows or locks, for example, on a MFH.
- SFHs are often slightly less conveniently located than MFHs, which may affect your ability to find tenants. SFHs are usually slightly further away from main roads and public transportation, retail shops, offices, and other places that your tenant may want to be close to. This is because MFHs are generally built in higher density areas, and higher density areas are built around shopping, offices, etc.

Contrast the above with the advantages and disadvantages of investing in Multi-Family Homes....

ADVANTAGES OF INVESTING IN MULTI-FAMILY HOMES

- Potential to cash flow better because there are typically many more units purchased for a slightly lower price per unit.
- More than one rent to help cover your operating costs – if one unit is vacant, there are other units bringing in revenue to help you out.
- Often a broader range of possible tenants to choose from as the per-unit rental cost is usually less than that of a SFH.
- If one unit becomes vacant, you can work on it (paint, put in new floors, etc.) but still be collecting rent from your other units/tenants.
- Economies of scale: for instance, your PM will likely charge you less (as a percentage of the rent) on a MFH than he/she will on a SFH. Furthermore, your utility costs will likely not be three times the amount (if it's a 3-unit MFH), even though there are three tenants living there.
- On a per unit basis, MFHs are less expensive than SFHs.
- Generally, your rent-to-price ratio is higher with MFHs than with SFHs (and this can often equate to more cash flow).

DISADVANTAGES OF INVESTING IN MULTI-FAMILY HOMES

Well, you can pretty much figure them out based on all of the above, but here's a quick list anyway!

- Maintenance tends to be higher, as there is often more wear and tear due to more people living in the building, more appliances to service/replace, and typically more tenant turnover.
- Tenant placement costs tend to be higher as MFHs often

have more turnover than SFHs. I don't have stats on this; it's just based on our personal experience.

- MFHs tend to appreciate slightly slower than SFHs.
- More limited buyer pool when it's time to sell.
- May take a lot longer to sell because of the limited buyer pool.
- Two words: Tenant squabbles!
- And financing can be more onerous.

From the advantages and disadvantages, you can see there are plenty of reasons for and against each type, so let's give you a real life example of SFH vs. MFH and you can decide which is the better buy!

For this example, we are comparing two Single Family Homes to one Multi-Family Home (a side-by-side duplex). The reason we are comparing 2 SFHs with 1 MFH is based on purchasing power. Basically, if you have x number of dollars to spend, you want to be able to compare based on that amount – rather than looking at, for example, $400,000 for a MFH vs. $300,000 for a SFH.

HERE'S OUR REAL LIFE CASE STUDY ON BUYING SINGLE FAMILY HOMES VS. MULTI-FAMILY HOMES:

Bought 2 SFH properties:	Bought 1 MFH (side-by-side duplex):
1 – $74,500; rent was $720 per month 2 – $72,500; rent was $500 per month	1 – $152,900; rent was $1,600 per month
Total cost: $147,000; total rent was $1,220 per month Total expenses on these two were $1,200 per month Net cash flow of an exciting $20 per month! Today's value: Total of $330,000 Total rent today: Total of $1,348 Total expenses: Total of $1,400 per month Currently a net loss of $52 per month!	Total expenses were $1,300 per month Net cash flow of $300 per month!! Today's value: $350,000 Today's rent: $2,450 Total expenses: $1,900 (after refinancing) Net cash flow of $550 per month!

So ... which one do you think is the better investment?

Well, in most cases, I would think our savvy readers would choose the MFH property as the better investment. And for some of you, it would be. However, there are a few reasons why I am not so sure that the MFH is the clear winner. Let me explain why...

1. The 2 SFHs are in a prime development area; thus the LAND value continues to go up and up and up! So the opportunity for good appreciation is stronger in that area than where the MFH is located.
2. The 2 SFHs are on freehold land whereas the MFH is in a strata community. There tend to be more restrictions on what you can and cannot do in a strata community vs. when you own the land on freehold title.
3. We have had a total of only four different tenants in the two SFHs over five years! One of our tenants has not changed since we bought it, and the other property has had three different families over the five years. Meanwhile, our MFH, although it is a pretty nice duplex, has had eight turnovers in the same timeframe. Higher turnover means higher placement costs, higher maintenance costs, and more stress!

So, the reason I share this example with you is to give you a taste of the fact that there often is *no clear winner* between SFHs and MFHs when it comes to real estate investing! What matters isn't which one is a better investment, but which one is a better investment for *your time, energy and resources.*

Before deciding that Multi-Family Homes are the better investment because they have the potential for better cash flow, first ask yourself these questions:

1. Who will be responding to any potential tenant squabbles (me or a professional Property Manager)?

2. Does the MFH have legal or illegal suites? If they're illegal (which many are), prepare yourself for the fact that if a noisy neighbour complains, you may have to work with the City to either legalize the suite (which can be costly) or decommission it. Either way, this may eat up a chunk of your time, energy, and money.

3. Who's going to be paying all the heat, hydro, and electricity bills? Are you going to pay and build it into the rent or is your plan to have your tenants each pay a portion? If you don't have each suite set up with a separate meter this can become a challenging issue for you and a point of contention for your tenants. Lots of tenants will complain about the usage of the other tenants if they have to split costs with each other.

And before deciding that Single Family Homes are the way to go, ask yourself these questions:

1. Can I carry the costs (mortgage, electricity, taxes, insurance, etc.) if there are vacancies?
2. Do I want to pay a Property Manager to manage just one tenant, or can I handle the odd late night repair phone call and some minor maintenance issues?
3. Do I strive for more liquidity in my investments (the ability to sell faster)?
4. Do I want the potential for greater appreciation or just monthly cash flow?

So in summary, figuring out which is the best strategy for *you* means digging into what type of property suits you best – rather than listening to all the "talkers" out there regarding which is the better investment. And yes, that even includes *yours truly*!

Living for Free (or really cheap): A Strategy for Buying Duplexes, Triplexes and Fourplexes

Looking for a way to buy a home to live in without having to carry a giant mortgage on your own income? Buy a multi-unit property like a duplex, triplex or fourplex. A well chosen property can find you living in a much better area than you could have afforded otherwise and paying a lot less "rent" than you would have otherwise done. We did this in Toronto for a few years. We moved into a three-unit property that we owned. Our friends moved into the top floor; we lived on the main floor; and we rented out the basement to some university students. Our "rent" was cheap; parts of our home expenses were a write–off, thanks to the rental income; and we got to live in the very desirable Little Italy area of Toronto, only minutes from a subway stop. A five-minute walk and we were in the heart of Little Italy shopping, dining and lounging. A five-minute walk the other way and we were on the subway and heading to downtown Toronto 15 minutes away. We were also right across the street from a large off-leash dog park (which our dog Bram would stare at longingly as he sat in front of the window.)

The major drawback of living in your multiple unit rental is that the burden of managing the property and dealing with the tenants can consume you. At one point while we were living in this property, our tenants in the basement were constantly fighting. We tell the whole story later in this book, but we were often being called in to play referee until one morning at 3 a.m. it all came to a climax when one of the basement tenants pulled out a butter knife and threatened her roommate with it. The tenant without the knife was terrified, called the police, and moved out in the morning.

The knife wielding tenant stayed in our basement for two months after this but stopped paying rent. Imagine the joy we felt living above an unstable tenant who also wasn't paying rent.

And worse for us was the fact that we could have avoided all of this by making better tenant choices – a subject we will also discuss later in the book.

The point here is to let you know that there are tremendous advantages *and* disadvantages to living in your investment property while renting out the other units to tenants. Nevertheless, as noted in the article above, small residential properties with two, three or four units are a great option to consider.

There is one other important thing to note if you do decide to live in a property that has been a rental or will be a rental for you. *If you decide to call it your primary residence and want to be able to sell it without paying capital gains taxes, you cannot depreciate it when it's a rental.* Plus you want to get clear on what you can and should write off, and how you can determine values for when it's your own home versus a rental. A few hundred dollars spent on good advice could save you thousands in taxes.

RECREATIONAL PROPERTIES

For years we wanted to buy a condo at Whistler Mountain, the world class ski resort two hours outside of Vancouver, British Columbia (and host of the 2010 Winter Olympics). We loved everything about Whistler, except the real estate prices. Finally, after spending nearly five years researching and working towards it, we settled on purchasing a quarter share of a large two-bedroom condo at Whistler in December 2010. It's not, however, an investment; in our minds it's a lifestyle purchase.

There are so many considerations involved in the purchase of a recreational property and it's more complex than we'll cover here. *The number of options, the fees to watch out for, the risks involved, and the benefits are completely different than when you're purchasing a regular investment property.* For us, the purchase of the Whistler property is to have our own place to use for skiing and mountain biking. Our ownership costs will be somewhat offset by rent, but the truth is we will be using it more than renting it out, so the rent we earn will be minimal. Over time the value *may* appreciate, but Whistler values have been steadily declining for nearly a decade so we don't expect to make money on it. We just plan to enjoy ourselves and recover as much of our costs as possible over time.

A couple of notes for you: Watch out for fees! Property management of a recreational property can be very expensive (50% of your income from the property in many places like Whistler is very common), and if you don't live nearby, you'll likely want to hire property management. Vandalism and other petty crimes can be a problem if someone isn't watching over the property. It's also much more difficult to rent it out if you haven't hired a property manager. The second issue is that financing can be very difficult as your own income often has to carry the property; it's nearly impossible if you buy something like a quarter share. Lenders just don't like things that are a little different. We had to go to a credit union that works with quarter shares and it was expensive! Some people make a lot of money on recreational property investing, but for the purposes of this workbook, we're going to focus your attention on single family homes, duplexes, triplexes and fourplexes.

THE KEY TO GOOD DEALS IN ALL MARKETS: BECOME A SUBMARKET EXPERT

In 2012, three of the deals we did came to *us*. The first one was a deal we tried to do in 2011 but we weren't willing to pay the price the sellers wanted. The second one was a house our neighbour sold to us. And the third one was from a marketing campaign we had done several years before.

When we tell people this, everyone comments on the fact that we're in magazines, everywhere online, and well known in local real estate circles so it makes sense that deals find us, but none of those deals came to us because of any sort of "fame" we have. Each of those deals came to us because we're *area experts* and we've taken steps to let people know where we buy and what houses we'd be interested in. We don't even look at deals beyond a few areas in Nanaimo, let alone in other cities. It simplifies everything we do *and* it allows us to get deeply entrenched into the areas where we want to buy so people can bring deals to *us*.

Once you've picked your property type and your market, choosing a *submarket* and becoming the known expert investor for that area is the secret sauce that takes your investments to the highest level without you having to dedicate all your waking hours to finding great deals.

This part takes work and time – and when I say *time* I definitely mean more time than two hours on MLS in the evening – but once you've invested the hours into building a foundation, it doesn't take much work to stay on top of things in your submarket and spot the money making deals. And it won't be that many years before deals come to you too!

One of our coaching clients was struggling with the concept of being a submarket area expert. He felt that it was too narrow. He wrote us after a couple of months of working on it and he said, "I was stuck – not really getting how narrowing my focus so much was going to help me. I kept with it, but I was getting frustrated. Then it just clicked. I started seeing deals. They were always there, but all of a sudden I could actually *see* them."

To become a submarket expert, you need to see a lot of homes. I've heard some experts say you won't know a great deal until you've seen 100 homes. That's a daunting number, and I don't think you have to see 100 homes before you do your first deal. But once you have that level of expertise in an area, finding great deals becomes much easier. If we were to take you on a drive in our target neighbourhood, we could tell you stories about every other home in the area because we've been in many of them, met the sellers, or seen what's been happening over the years. There's one street in Nanaimo where we have owned four homes (we only own two on that street right now because tenants bought the other two in rent to own deals). As you can imagine, if a home goes for sale on "our" street, we go to see it. And when we did our marketing campaigns, that street heard from us a lot. In 2010, 2011 and the start of 2012, we were buying a house a month without blinking and the only reason that worked for us was because we only did it in a couple of neighbourhoods.

HOW TO BECOME AN AREA EXPERT

To start gaining market area knowledge, walk around the area and make note of "For Rent" signs, calling to learn more (price, amenities, anything they emphasize); and then keep checking back to make a note of when the sign comes down. Be on the lookout for "For Sale" signs and do the same thing. Go to Open Houses. Speak with local real estate agents. Speak with local property managers. You can even chat with people you see on the street. The whole time try to find out:

- Who is a typical home owner in this area?
- Where do people work?
- Where do the kids go to school?
- *What do you like best about this area?*
- *Anything to watch out for in this area?*
- *What would my target property type rent out for?*

And, of course, collect the "Property Sold" data for the area. Most real estate agents have a system whereby they can send you an email when a new listing, a price change, or a home sale occurs in your target area. This is enormously useful for keeping tabs on the market activity.

Once you've got your submarket picked out, and you've dedicated time to getting a strong sense of who lives in that area and why, the house prices, the rent rates, the amenities in a home that are important to buyers and renters, the things that make a house in that area harder to sell or rent – and you've physically seen at least a dozen of your target type homes – all you need to do is monitor the area.

Just because you don't see deals right away doesn't mean there aren't deals there.

We have had points in time in the last 18 months where we've looked at dozens of houses and made at least six offers before we get a deal that meets our criteria. And we're intensely focused, full time real estate investors with a lot of time and resources dedicated to uncovering deals.

Most of the time we find a deal or two each month that works for us, but sometimes you have to be patient. Nevertheless, there are things you can do, besides waiting for an MLS listing that fits your criteria, to find deals faster:

1. Call FSBO (for sale by owner) listings you see advertised. Generally we find FSBO homes are overpriced and the owners not that motivated to sell, but every once in awhile you can find a great deal. In the last few years, many of the FSBO deals that we have looked at have been overpriced because the owner owed more than the house was worth or they were just feeling out the market before they listed it and weren't that motivated. One of the deals we did in 2012 was first an FSBO that we tried to buy. The seller didn't agree to our price and then listed it shortly after we'd made our offer. We waited a month and then bought it for the same price we'd offered him privately. Once he'd consulted with a realtor and put it on the market, he was willing to accept that our price was a decent offer, but before that he thought he could do better. We still try with FSBO's but they aren't our best source of deals.

2. Call for-rent advertisements not posted by a professional property management company. You may find tired landlords who would love to partner with you, or else sell you their property that they can't seem to find tenants for because they aren't targeting the right tenants (and you know who to target because you're a sub-market expert now!). One of the deals we did in 2010 was with a couple that wanted to spend six months a year travelling – so they didn't want to manage their rental, nor could they sell their property for a price they were happy with, and nor were they happy with local property management options. So we partnered with them on their property based on its appraised value that day. We became 50-50

partners. We made them money on their property and took care of it so they didn't have to worry; and we got into the deal with nothing more than the cost of an appraisal and a joint venture agreement.

3. Go to your local real estate club meetings – this has been a tremendous source of deals, joint venture money and private lenders for us. The first RRSP mortgage we did was with folks who approached us at a Nanaimo Real Estate Club meeting. One of our coaching clients found a property in Victoria to flip through someone she met at a club meeting in her city. Another one of our coaching clients found his first JV partner and a great deal at a club meeting in Surrey.

4. When you are meeting people in the area, mention that you're interested in buying. Jot your number on a piece of paper so they can get in touch with you if they know someone. If you have a dog or a child to walk around with you, you'll typically get into more conversations with people. We've had so many leads come to us just because people know we buy houses on that street.

5. Let other people know you're shopping in that area: real estate agents, property managers, trades people you know. Even our junk removal company brings us leads.

6. You can do very low cost online marketing to target sellers in your area. You'll find that you'll get a wide variety of responses, so keep your focus on your target property type and your target area and don't get distracted. You can try Yellow Letter Marketing to specific houses, flyers, business cards in mailboxes, and more, depending on your budget. Our coaching client Michelle Pink of http://thinkpinkrealestate.ca/ put an ad in her neighbourhood paper in Calgary. It had a picture of her with her family. When she took her son to his playgroup, people started asking her about what she did and what kinds of houses she bought. It hasn't resulted in a deal at this point, but it's building awareness of what she does in her target area and will likely pay dividends in the near future.

We'll come back to some of these strategies later in the book, but the big thing is to *consistently* do a few things each week. Over time, the deals will become so obvious it will be like there is a neon sign saying "GREAT DEAL HERE." And, even better, because you're a sub-market expert, you'll know exactly what to say in your ad when you go to put tenants in your suite, and you'll rarely find yourself dealing with a vacancy.

It sounds straightforward – because it is.

There are other benefits to getting to know the neighbourhood ... like ease of finding and hiring trades people; how neighbours and other people quickly know what deals you're looking for and send them your way; tenants that will tell other people about you because you have houses in the area, and so much more!

Most of our properties get a higher than average rent rate because we have the exact house tenants are looking for and we offer it in great condition. As a result, we have tenants that take care of our properties, stay longer and make us more money with fewer hassles.

Want to learn exactly how we do that? Well ... keep reading!!

THE POWER OF BEING AN AREA EXPERT

At the end of 2010, we closed on a property that we bought for $40,000 under its market value – and guess how much work we had to do to it? A few thousand dollars. We had to put in two baseboard heaters and paint two bedrooms. That was it! It was in immaculate condition.

When our inspector walked in, he said, "You paid *what* for this???" After he inspected it and found out it was in excellent condition, he had to ask us: "Why so cheap??"

He couldn't believe that we got such a bargain on such a high-end home in a great area ... and the part that is even more unbelievable for most people is that we bought this property off MLS. What I am explaining here is how we get deals like this – right off MLS.

It had been on the market for over a year. It started with a listing price of $429,000. It didn't even hit my radar until it went down to $359,000; and even then it was only because it was in one of our three main submarkets – we like to see all the homes that come on the market in those three areas that meet our criteria for size, etc. When the price dropped to $349,000, we went to see the home and we agreed it was probably worth that price; but it wasn't within walking distance of schools or shopping ... it was a few minutes' drive away ... so we weren't that interested. Besides, $349,000 is at the high end of what we'll pay for a home and we rarely go that high.

It dropped to $329,000 and I was more interested, but we were busy with a couple of other deals at the time so I didn't concern myself with it. Then I saw it make two drops in a short period of time and hit $314,900. At that price, it was a steal ... plus with two big drops in a week I knew the sellers were finally ready to deal after over a year of trying to sell their property. We didn't need to see it again. I quickly made an offer and it was a quick negotiation.

The very day our offer was accepted, the home was shown something like eight times. It had been on the market so long that it had been ignored; but the new low price of $314,900 finally got people's attention. It was shown so much the next few days that the listing agent took the lock box down because she was tired of showing it.

Fortunately, we had been fast enough that we got in before people realized what a deal it was. We ended up getting it for $303,000. The appraisal came in at $328,000, but everyone that has seen it agrees that it's worth at least $340,000.

We now have great tenants in that home, putting a small amount of cash in our pockets each month (it is positive cash flowing by only a few hundred a month), and when we sell someday we'll have a whole lot of extra equity to cash out.

Before I go any further, I want to let you know that we have a couple of resources to help you out. Head on over to: **www.revnyou.com**

Look for the image of the book and click where it says "Register My Book."

When you register, you'll be signed up for our newsletter, and with it you'll receive a handful of resources to supplement what we've been talking about in this book:

- A simple spreadsheet to help you calculate cash flow on your properties;
- A cheat sheet outlining the formula for buying properties with a CAUSE;
- Plus a few other resources I'll talk about later in the book.

FINDING DEALS WITH MARKETING

Some investors cover their cars in decals, letting everyone know they are an investor. (I hope they never cut anyone off or make driving mistakes though – everyone will know it was them!) Other investors spend a lot of money on marketing. We've done that. In an 18-month period we invested about $17,000 on a giant marketing campaign that included magnets, bus bench ads, flyers and a big direct marketing campaign. Here's how that worked out for us:

OUR MASSIVE "YELLOW LETTER" MARKETING CAMPAIGN

As I watched Dave race up one of the many hills in St. John's, Newfoundland en route to Ryan Mansion where we were staying, I wished I had our Flip camera handy. It felt like we were on our very own episode of **Amazing Race: The Real Estate Investing** version.

After months of research, property tours, and more research, we had uncovered two real estate gems. One was a duplex and the other a single family home. Neither property was distressed but they were both very solid deals.

So ... we decided to buy them both. Everything was going

along just fine until we encountered a little glitch with our partner. We had closed on a deal with him a few months earlier so we didn't think there would be any problems getting a mortgage for the property with him on title. Unfortunately the entire lending landscape changed that year, and the main program that had been in place, the one that had worked to qualify him for deals, was no longer available.

No problem – we figured we'd just find a couple of new partners. Except the people we were contacting had less than 48 hours to make their decision before we took off on vacation. When you're asking people for $50,000, they generally want more than 48 hours to think about it ... even when the deals are compelling – which they were!

We worked the phones for two solid days, determined to find people to join us on these two deals. And ... with only a few days to spare before we had to remove any conditions, we found two new partners with the cash to do the deals. But we were still hitting issues with the banks. We had to extend the conditions on the deals for four business days and keep working the deals. That meant we were running around St. John's trying to get things signed, faxed and couriered to the appropriate people.

We were in St. John's for our friends' wedding and unfortunately didn't really get to enjoy most of our vacation because we spent the better part of our 10-day vacation glued to the phone trying to save the two deals.

What had been working well for us in the past for many of our deals didn't work anymore and we felt so frustrated. We decided to change our investing strategies so we didn't have to rely on banks and other people's money all the time. We started to focus our attention on attracting motivated sellers. The idea was that we would find people who were willing to sell us their house creatively, using options that do not require a bank to finance the deal – options such as:

- Wrap-around mortgages
- Agreements for sale

- Lease options
- Seller financing.

Right around the same time, a U.S. investment guru was coming to Edmonton to share his expertise. His entire program was about finding motivated sellers so you could put together creative deals, and this was exactly what we were looking for.

After his three-day course in Edmonton, we set to work. The plan we chose focused on covering a couple of select areas in Nanaimo, BC with bright orange business cards, orange and black magnets, online ads, and flyers in newspapers. The foundation of our campaign, however, was the Yellow Letter Marketing.

The only snag in our plan was cost. We were looking at a $10,000 investment to produce everything, not even counting the fact that we had to have someone to answer our phone once all the leads started coming in. We were willing to invest that kind of capital into growing our business, but our concern was how much the "per call" costs could run us.

My Dad, an active commercial real estate investor for over 30 years, went to the course with Dave. He was pretty excited about our plans to market to Nanaimo home owners, and he offered to partner with us. Instead of us paying a company that specializes in handling these types of calls at $1 per call, plus $1 per minute to take messages; Dad offered to handle the calls on the spot and become our partner in all the deals.

SETTING UP OUR YELLOW LETTER MARKETING CAMPAIGN

Once Dad agreed to be our answering service, Mom offered to coordinate the creation of the letters. Next:

1. We found a list company from which to purchase our mailing list. We paid $1,500 for a list of approximately 6,800 names in specific postal codes in the city of Nanaimo.
2. We photocopied our handwritten letter that basically

said, "Hi, my name is Rick. My wife Ruth-Anne and I are interested in buying your house at 123 Lovely Street. Please call us at 250-555-5555." We hired a handful of people to assist with writing the home owner's first name and their home address on the letters, hand writing the addresses on the envelopes, and sticking on stamps. We paid 20 cents for each letter and 30 cents for each completed envelope, plus the 52 cents for the stamp.

3. We set up a separate phone line at Mom and Dad's house so the calls would be separate from their personal and business line.

4. We prepared my Dad with plenty of lead sheets to complete while chatting with the people who called in. Each sheet had a list of questions he would need to ask so that he could get the important information about their houses for us to decide if we wanted to buy them. We also set up a tracking system so we could track who responded and who didn't, who asked not to be contacted again, and who would need to be followed up with at a later date.

5. Starting in early November 2009, we began mailing the letters out at a rate of 250 per week.

THE IMMEDIATE RESULTS OF THE CAMPAIGN

We ran bus bench ads, placed newspaper ads, ran online promos, distributed flyers through newspapers, put magnets on mail boxes, and handed out hundreds of "we buy houses" business cards in a 12-month period. No other marketing method we tested came close to the response we received from the Yellow Letters. Within 48 hours of the first batch of letters hitting the post office, Dad's phone was ringing off the hook. He walked around with a headset on and chatted happily to the curious, confused, angry or scared folks that called in.

From the first 2,000 letters we mailed out, we had a 30-40% response rate. That is, for every 10 people that received a letter, we were getting 3 to 4 calls!

A lot of callers were on guard when they first called. They were defensive and wanted to know how he got their name. They were scared that it was a scam. They were curious but concerned.

My Dad was brilliant at disarming folks and making them comfortable. When someone would skeptically ask him, "What are you up to?" he would say, "I'm up to about 5'9" and 185 pounds, but I'm trying to lose some weight!"

It was early in our days of shooting video, but we did capture some of the funny stories that my Dad told. You can find them on our YouTube channel at

www.youtube.com/revnyou

With Dad's humour, people generally relaxed, and then he was able to find out whether they had a house they were interested in selling or not. He had some wonderful conversations with people and thoroughly enjoyed himself most of the time. He even had an invitation to come out and see a guy's race cars, invitations to come and see homes even though they weren't for sale, and dozens and dozens of people who said they would hang on to the letter and call us first when they were ready to sell.

IT WAS MOSTLY FUN UNTIL THE POLICE WERE CALLED

Not everyone was comfortable with what we were doing. A small percentage of the calls my Dad received were from very hostile people who felt we were targeting elderly people or the families of someone who had just passed away. We began to receive the odd letter from someone's lawyer asking us to "cease and desist" contact with their client. At least a dozen people called the local police. That resulted in one call from the police to investigate what we were doing and another call a month or so later acknowledging that while we weren't doing anything wrong, they would appreciate it if we stopped because they were still getting complaints.

Of course it didn't take long before the local newspaper got wind of what we were doing and ran a story on it as well. It was full of negative commentary about what we were doing, but it did include a statement from the police that we were not doing anything illegal.

For the most part, it was entertaining; but there were days where it was emotionally draining for my Dad. Especially when two months into it, and nearly 500 calls later, we hadn't found a single person willing to sell their home "creatively." In fact, we actually uncovered a lot of people who had paid off their home fully and weren't moving until nature made them.

Eventually we started to speak with some folks that were very interested and willing to sell creatively. When a lead like this came in, Dave and I would head out to view the home and meet with the seller. What we discovered in each of these cases was that:

- The house was in a terrible area; and/or
- The home needed way too much work and wasn't worth what they were asking, given the work required; and/or
- The seller wanted at least 20% more than the home was actually worth.

In every case where we found someone willing to be creative with their deal, that person wanted a grotesque amount of money for their property or the property was one we didn't want to deal with. We began to think we were doing something wrong! We figured we must be missing something important, so we went back over all the leads that had come in (nearly 1,000 by this time) and followed up on some of them to make sure we hadn't missed an opportunity. If we had, we were still missing it. There were deals in that pile for the person with the right expertise and resources to handle bad areas and ugly properties, but that was not us.

It took almost four months before we found a deal we wanted to do – and even then it was not a creative deal. It was simply an awesome house in a great area that we could buy with $30,000 of equity in it. If we wanted to finance it without a bank, it was going to be through private money – not through creative techniques like an agreement for sale or a VTB (vendor take back) mortgage. But for a house that didn't need any work, in a great and centrally located area of town, we grabbed the deal and worried about the money afterwards.

The second deal that came through our yellow letter campaign was a deal similar to the first – in that it was a good house, in a good area, and we could buy it with about $30,000 in equity in the home. We grabbed it too. We solved our financing challenges by finding joint venture partners that could qualify for financing and provide the capital.

THE RETURN ON INVESTMENT

Sticking to the initial campaign, which cost us about $12,000, and hundreds of hours of my Dad's time, and dozens of hours of our time, our return on investment was definitely low. We didn't do *any* creative deals – which is what we set out to do in the first place. But we did manage to pick up two great properties in six months with $60,000 in equity and a combined total of $900 per month in positive cash flow. Not a bad result, but not the result we were going for.

In 2012 we closed on a property assessed at $400,000. We paid $320,000 for it. The owner had received our letter and held onto it for two years until she was ready to sell. The house was in our favorite neighbourhood and was perfect for putting in suites – so that is what we've done.

The yellow letters were the *only* marketing we did that gave us a return on our investment. (We did receive a few calls from our bus bench ads, online ads and flyers, but the response was very small and none of those calls resulted in leads we were interested in).

Because there was so much negativity around the letters, in a later mailing that we did in mid-2010, we tried to change the wording a bit to make it clear that we were investors interested in buying their home. (Before that, the letter had only given our name and said that we were interested in buying their house at 123 Street). We also sat down and went through our list line by line and hand-picked very specific houses to send the letters to. It took dramatically more work to put together the list for mailing, and our response rate dropped to under 10%. We didn't do any deals from those letters.

LESSONS FOR YELLOW LETTER CAMPAIGNS

Yellow letters are a great tool to generate targeted leads and also learn a whole lot about the community you are investing in; but, as described, there are big challenges. I don't think this strategy is right for very many investors, but if you decide to tackle creating a yellow letter campaign, here are a few suggestions:

- Mailing lists are expensive and they go stale fast, so get yourself organized and ready before you order the list.
- Figure out how you'll handle the calls. If you're going to take the calls yourself, set up a separate phone line that you can turn off. Some people called my dad in the middle of the night! Another option is to just set up a voicemail account like evoice.com. All the calls will go to voicemail and you may lose some leads; but if someone *really* wants to sell, they will leave you a message. Also, you may want to consider outsourcing this to a country with good English and low wage costs, like the Philippines. We work with high quality folks from the Philippines in our business and this is how we would handle a campaign like this if we were to do it today. Successful wholesalers we know in Alberta use a team from the Philippines that they have trained to screen the leads. It took them time to find good people and train them, but at least they don't waste time on possible deals that don't meet their specific criteria.

- Know what types of deals you are willing to do. Just because a house is cheap or a seller will work with you on a creative deal does not make it a good opportunity.
- Prepare yourself for all kinds of responses. Some people will be furious with you. My Dad was caught off guard because some people were very angry. We didn't expect that kind of response and at times it was draining. Expect it, and get ready to brush it off and move on.
- Be polite and friendly to everyone – some of our best leads from that campaign came via people who gave our name to a friend or family member that was selling.
- Be patient. It's not overnight. Nothing in life, or real estate, is.

CHAPTER SIX

ANALYZING REAL ESTATE DEALS

W e've been to some real estate programs where they promise you can do deals from the comfort of your own home. "All you need is a computer, internet access and a telephone and you're in business," they suggest. No matter how great technology gets there is nothing that replaces actually being there, smelling the house, and seeing the area first hand. There is a lot more to analyzing a property than just running numbers – no matter what your exit plan is.

Have you ever watched Dragons' Den or Shark Tank (the U.S. version)? Both shows are entertaining but they are also educational if you pay attention to the questions the dragons and sharks ask and the observations they make.

It's never just about the return they can make on their money.

Let's take Kevin O'Leary as an example because he's the most black and white when it comes to the subject of risk versus reward. Other Dragons may invest for reasons extending beyond risk and return, but he doesn't. For him, it's always about making money. He's entertaining, obnoxious and single-minded in his investment strategies (or the show has been created to make him appear that way).

He often refers to his dollars as soldiers. He sends them out to battle *only* in the highest likelihood they will win and return with more soldiers. As in any battle, it's inevitable that a few will die, but he wants to kill as few as possible. In his mind, that's murder.

His point is: *focus on the end when you start.* What's the likelihood that you'll get your money back – with a return – at the end?

What could happen that could cause your soldiers to die at war? Those are the risks you are going to be taking. What you'll find is: the higher the potential profits and rewards, the higher the risks are that you'll lose your money.

Real estate development is one of those businesses. The returns the developers are usually looking at are 20-30%. They build that right into their pro forma at the beginning to make sure it's in the deal for them (at least that is what I was taught when I did my MBA in real estate a decade ago ... times may have changed). It sounds like a great return until you start analyzing *all* the things that could go wrong to cause them to potentially lose that profit and possibly lose additional money.

One of my colleagues from my MBA days who got into development tells a crazy story of how he tried to get a piece of land subdivided. Between backhoes stuck in the mud, neighbours with shot guns urinating on his property while he was touring investors around, unexpected legal costs, and challenges with city officials, his project cost him six figures *more* than he had budgeted for. It was a nightmare, and if the market had been flat or declining he would have lost over $100,000 – which was money he did not have at the time. The *only* reason he ended up profiting on that project was because it was during a time in the mid 2000's when prices were skyrocketing. The price of his land shot up significantly in the 18 months it took to develop that piece of land to the point where builders could build on it.

Flipping is also high risk because you can find unexpected issues when you go to renovate (you *never* really know what's behind the walls until you get there); or the market can unexpectedly shift down a bit – enough to erode your profits. Both challenges are out of your control and can completely ruin a deal.

It doesn't mean you shouldn't develop or flip, but it does mean you really need to know what you're doing because the margin of error gets much larger. *Your returns can go up but your risks do too.*

What we've settled on for the bulk of our investment activities is what I would call a bread-and-butter approach. It's basic. It's easily repeatable. It's lower risk and it's less stressful. The returns are good but they aren't as large as some other strategies and they take time to materialize.

ANALYZING THE NUMBERS ON A PROPERTY

There are many approaches to analyzing the cash flow on a property.

Dave approaches it very systematically – running numbers on a spreadsheet. He tests for interest rate fluctuations, potential rent rate changes, and other factors that could greatly impact our returns.

I walk into a property and can figure out whether we should buy it in about sixty seconds. I can quickly guesstimate what the rent we can get is (remember – we're area experts, so I know what rents for what price in this area off the top of my head); and I know the price range within which I can buy this place and make it work because we've done so many deals.

I also get a *feeling* from a property. I will tell you more about this intuition that I have later in the book – because you probably have it too and don't even know it yet!

*Part of finding a property is **evaluation**. You are looking for the property that is going to meet your goals. To achieve that, you'll need to be able to analyze and value the property and figure out if it's going to make you money.*

Your job as you evaluate specific properties is to disregard the list price or what the sellers may want for it and focus solely on what it's worth to you!

- What's the property worth based on the cash flow?
- What's the property worth based on comparables?
- What's the property worth based on replacement value?

Don't worry about the city's property assessment or about what the sellers paid for it. Those numbers are mostly irrelevant. You may be able to use them in your negotiation if it comes to that, but for the purposes of evaluating the property they're not important.

As you look at the property, consider the following:

- What is the area zoned for? (What else can you do with it? Can you add retail or office space or additional units?). What is its highest and best use?
- Are there any restrictions on the use of the property?
- What is the immediate area like? Are the other houses well maintained or not? Are there parks?
- What is in the area that is attractive for someone living there? Schools, shopping, medical services, police/fire and other services?
- What kind of transportation options are within a few blocks?
- What condition is the property in? Exterior and interior?
- *What is your gut telling you* when you see the property? How do you feel when you're in the property?
- Are there easy things you can do to improve the appearance of the property?
- Are there any environmental risks to consider? Earthquakes, hurricanes, mold, termites, asbestos, bed bugs, etc.?
- Who lives there now? Tenants or the owners?

Some of these things you can be assessed using maps and information you can gather from the internet, but most of these questions require you to physically be there to properly answer them.

Then, to figure out values, you'll need to do the same evaluation for other properties that are on the market, as well as those that have recently sold in the area. You'll also have to spend some time figuring out what kind of rent rate you can get for the property.

If two properties are comparable in size and location, yet one property (on a dollar per sq. ft. basis) is much more expensive or much cheaper, it's your job to figure out *why*. The cheaper property may be in a slightly worse location. Or it could be on a noisier street, or near a garbage dump, or in a position where it gets less sun, etc. These are some of the things you'll need to determine to figure out value and possible rent rates.

A RULE OF THUMB TO HELP YOU ESTIMATE EXPENSES

Most rental properties have expenses of at least 35% of the rental revenue. This can include property taxes, house insurance, property management, maintenance, materials, water/sewage/garbage, etc. So it's helpful if you give yourself a buffer of at least 35% to pay for expenses. This will leave you 60-70% of rental income to pay for financing costs (and, if planned well, some cash in your pocket each month!).

If you are doing a rent-to-own, your expenses are lower because the tenants are responsible for more of the expenses. About 20% is more accurate for a rent to own. You'll still pay for house insurance and taxes, but you probably won't have a property manager. You'll have less maintenance, and your tenant will typically pay for water/sewage/garbage.

CALCULATING CASH FLOW

At this point in your evaluation of properties, you likely have enough information to get a clear picture of whether your potential properties will have positive cash flow.

So what do you need to know to further evaluate your properties? Gather most of the following information to calculate cash flow:

- Rent
- Property taxes
- Heat/hydro (and who pays for it – the potential tenant or the owner?)
- Electricity (again, who pays for it?)
- Garbage/sewer/recycling fees
- Property insurance (you can speak with an Insurance Broker for an estimate)
- Property management (again, you will want to research this to get an estimate)
- Maintenance of the building/property.

Separate from the above, you will want to come up with a rough idea of how much you will have for a down payment – so you can estimate your financing costs – and also get an estimate of the current interest rates. (You can check this online or speak to your bank or a mortgage broker.)

Many of the items above can be *estimated* until you have an accepted offer on the property, at which point you'll have easier access to the real numbers. However, the more *actuals* you can obtain from the seller (or seller's agent) and from your various sources (banker, broker, insurance agent, etc.), the more accurate your cash flow prediction will be!

WHENEVER WE BEGIN EVALUATING A PROPERTY, WE ALWAYS USE THE FOLLOWING RULE:

Income/Financing Ratio: 65% of income should be the maximum financing (mortgage principal and interest) cost.

E.g., *if rent is $2,000/month, financing should not exceed $1,300/ month (2,000 x .65 = $1,300).*

Even if you are going to manage the property yourself, it's always wise to have a buffer – in the event there comes a time where you can no longer manage the building yourself and need to hire a professional. Sometimes, when we've moved cities, changed to more demanding jobs, or just couldn't handle the strain and stress of managing the properties, we've gone from self-managing to professional management!

Knowing *only* the expenses won't help you if you haven't determined what rent you'll be getting. As we already discussed, it's imperative that you obtain accurate rental information in your chosen area and for comparable properties. A quick refresher:

USE THE FOLLOWING SOURCES TO OBTAIN COMPARABLE RENTS:

- www.rentometer.com (U.S.) or www.rentometer.com/ca
- http://kijiji.ca/
- www.craigslist.org
- Your local classifieds
- Drive by the area looking for FOR RENT signs on comparable properties. Call the number on the sign, or knock on the door (if the sign invites you to do so), then find out the rent and characteristics of the property.

At this point, we also *highly recommend* that you start connecting with at least one property management company in your area and ask them about rental rates. If you call them now, you can consider this as preliminary legwork for finding a good property manager when you buy the property! When you are speaking with them, you may even be able to find out the sizes, types, and locations of some of the properties they currently manage.

TIP: Always look for a property manager BEFORE you buy a property

Even if you're going to self-manage your property to begin with, you want to know that there is a professional who will take on your property if you need them. When Dave first began looking at investment properties in Niagara Falls, Ontario, he ran the numbers but didn't make sure there were reputable managers that would manage the properties. It wasn't until after the deals were done that he started to look for someone to help manage. He called every professional property manager in Niagara Falls, but after they drove by the properties, every single one of them refused to manage them. Dave ended up calling the seller and asking for a referral to the property manager he had worked with. That's how the manslaughter story and the crackhouse story began.

But the problem continued once we had to let that property manager go (after we discovered it was a known crackhouse in the area). Two years later and a newspaper article talking about it as a drug distribution center hadn't improved its appeal to professional property managers. We were about to move to BC from Ontario so we had to have help (especially since most tenants paid in cash). Dave ended up hiring a guy who wanted to get into property management. He had no experience and little expertise. I probably don't have to tell you how it worked out to have a guy with no skills managing a very high maintenance property with problem tenants.

Save yourself from the same experience by ensuring that you have options. If you're investing in a smaller market (i.e., markets like Barrie, Red Deer, Medicine Hat, Weyburn, Port Alberni, etc.), make sure that the folks in the property management business in your area will take on a property like the one you're about to buy.

Once you have done your research, you will have a decent range of rental incomes for comparable properties in your chosen area.

If your chosen property is already rented, then hopefully you were able to find out the current rent from the listing, the Listing Agent, or your Agent. Are the current tenants in a lease already, or is it just month to month? Asking the rent rate that the current tenants are paying is *not* enough research. It's entirely possible they are paying considerably more or considerably less for some other reason (family, friends, etc.)

> If the current tenants are paying **well below** market value, it is essential that you don't **jump** at the deal just because the Listing Agent (or Seller) says, "Oh, you can get way higher rent once these tenants move out!"

Tenants paying under market rents likely know they are getting a good deal, and chances are they may *never* move out! Secondly, in many states and provinces there are Rent Controls in place that only allow you to increase a tenant's rent by a regulated percentage each year (and that is usually a *maximum* of around 2-4%). If the tenants stay, you will *never* get up to market rent! Low rents can also be a good indicator of a poorly maintained property. If a landlord hasn't been generating much income from a property, they are less likely to spend money on repairs. These required repairs will be your problem when you try to raise the rents!

Properties that have "long-term tenants" who happen to be paying "below-market rents" can be troublesome.

The property may seem like a good deal because the average rental rate is much higher than what this property is generating. On paper, if you look at estimated rent using market rates, the deal will look good. Having tenants in place may save you a bit of time and effort having to find new ones, but if you can't make the property cash flow with them there, then you've got a whole bunch of other problems to deal with.

Don't get too excited by *potential*. Stick to your research and the current numbers. After thoroughly researching comparable rents in the area, does it look like the rental income will support a Gross Rent Multiplier (GRM) of around 10 (or up to 12)?

THE GRM FORMULA:

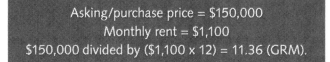

Asking/purchase price = $150,000
Monthly rent = $1,100
$150,000 divided by ($1,100 x 12) = 11.36 (GRM).

If there is not a current renter in place, you will want to use the average rent you found while doing your research.

Thus, if you have a range of $1,200 to $2,000 for comparable properties, you will want to use around $1,500 to $1,600 when estimating your GRM. This all depends on the quality and location of your property versus the other ones you are comparing it to.

Do not use the highest rent amount for your calculations! It's always best to be conservative when estimating rents!

HOW TO INCREASE THE CASH FLOW

For eight years we owned a triplex in the Little Italy area of Toronto. Two of the units were always rented and had long term tenants in them. In fact, when we sold the property, the upstairs tenants had lived in the property for over four years and as far as we heard last, they still live there! But the basement unit turned over at least once a year and it didn't fill very quickly. It was frustrating for us because the property was walking distance to the University and Hospital and steps away from the Christie subway station. In other words, it was a fantastic location and should have appealed to a wide variety of people.

One day in the middle of trying to fill the basement suite – again – we were walking down the street to get to the property. We were laughing and watching the dogs play at the park across the road and we started to talk about getting our own dog. A couple walking a cute lab type dog walked by us and we started asking questions about the dog. We asked the couple if they lived in the area. They said "We'd love to, but there aren't any rentals that take dogs, so we live north of here."

We understood all too well why many landlords don't want pets – we'd had a bad experience with a puppy in our first rental property. When we bought that property, we put brand new carpet in the living room and hallway. The tenant got a puppy without telling our property manager, and at some point thereafter she ended up going bankrupt and leaving abruptly.

The carpet was ruined – right through to the underlay – because the puppy had obviously repeatedly peed on the carpet. We had to replace the entire carpet – for the second time in less than a year. After that, all our rentals became pet-free.

Still, what the couple at the park had said stuck with us. We considered the fact that the basement suite didn't have any carpet and that making it pet friendly might increase our pool of renters ... so we took a leap and advertised it as "pet friendly."

That was the *only* change we made on the ad, but the showing a few days later was the busiest we'd ever had and we ended up with a bidding war on our hands. One applicant actually offered to bake us cookies every month if we would rent to her.

We put the rent up $100 per month and we never had a problem filling the property from that day until we sold.

I am not saying that taking pets is a sure-fire way to increase your rents – it *does* come with drawbacks – but in many areas it can be a tremendous way to increase your pool of renters *and* get a higher rent rate.

SO WHAT ELSE CAN YOU DO TO INCREASE RENT OR IMPROVE CASH FLOW?

If you have found a *great* property (location and building are great, close to schools, public transportation, good jobs, etc.), it's worth your time to see if you can make the deal work *despite* the lack of current cash flow.

You have a few opportunities here. Sometimes it depends on city rules (i.e., you might be able to add a suite but that may not be legal in your area) – but here are some simple ways to improve cash flow and a discussion of each one:

1. Increase rents
2. Add income from other sources
3. Pay less for the property
4. Reduce other expenses
5. Put up a larger down payment (to reduce your financing costs).

If your tenants are paying under-market rents, you can raise their rent – if a rental increase is allowed in your province or state. (You have to research your own market because the rules are different everywhere. Some provinces and states have rental restrictions so the amount you can raise rents and the frequency are limited.)

Keep in mind that a *large* increase may cause them to move out, or just be unhappy tenants that damage your property.

In general, we try not to charge the absolute maximum possible amount of rent because we want to keep our tenants for as long as possible. That said, the quality of home we offer, plus the fact that we offer pet friendly homes, typically means we get higher than normal rents.

It may seem confusing when I say "don't charge too much," but then say that we charge higher than normal rents. The big difference is that if you have a product that is hard to come by (high quality, pet friendly homes in great areas), you *will* be able to command higher rents; but the key is to not push it to the point where tenants are able to get something similar for less. *Tenant turnover is more expensive than getting $25 less per month in rent.*

Also, tenants that are paying slightly below market rent tend to be less demanding than tenants paying more than market rent. Think about it – if you know you are paying a premium for a place, are you going to change the light bulb yourself or are you going to call your landlord to make the change?

Finally, once you have done your rental research on the area, you may have identified features tenants will pay more for. An in-suite washer and dryers always adds value in our area. We can charge at least $100/month more if the unit has in-suite laundry. The challenge, of course, is how costly will it be to put one in. In other areas, air conditioning or covered parking may be the winning formula to get more rent.

ADD INCOME FROM OTHER SOURCES

Can you add storage, parking and/or even advertising to increase rents or draw income from another source? We know people who allow local trades to advertise on their lawn for an extra $50/month. Commercial buildings can sell space for antennas or signage. In Alberta, it's common to make $200/month additional for renting out a detached garage.

One fellow who attended our workshop on raising money has a business in Ontario where he's putting solar panels on the roofs of his rentals and selling that energy. It's turning into a very profitable business for him.

One of our primary strategies for increasing income is to add a legal suite to a property. It takes a significant investment (usually $60,000 - $75,000) but it usually results in us being able to get a total of $500/month more rent from a house than if we didn't have the suite and rented out the entire house to one family.

In our triplex in Toronto, we had coin-operated laundry machines that we'd purchased used. It was surprising how much money these machines brought in each year – sometimes as much as $500! Ask your fellow real estate investors what they do to generate additional income from their properties – you never know when you'll come across a great idea that you can implement.

PAY LESS FOR THE PROPERTY

We're going to get into negotiation strategies soon. For now, let me mention that when you make an offer to purchase, there is one condition you should almost always put in the deal. That is: *subject to an inspection.* This means the vendor has to give access to the property within a reasonable amount of time to complete an inspection.

What that inspection reveals can be used as leverage to reduce the purchase price or get work done that you would otherwise have to pay for. Basically, if the inspector comes back and tells you that the roof needs replacing or that the wiring is outdated, you can go back to the vendor and ask for a price reduction because of the work you are going to have to do. Sometimes the vendor will offer to get the work done, but our preference would *always* be to get it done ourselves. *If the vendor does opt to do the work, make sure you are told who will be doing the work (and that they are reputable) and get receipts and warranties for the completed work.*

We had a situation – last year, actually – where the inspection revealed a bunch of mold in the ceiling. We asked for a reduction in the selling price so we could have the problem remediated, but the seller said he would take care of it. He immediately got a company out and completed the work. Unfortunately, when we followed up on the work, we found out the company belonged to a friend of the sellers. That in itself wasn't a big deal because we checked into the reputation of the company and it was excellent. The big deal to us was the fact that the work was done under the table as a favor between friends; and therefore we had nothing to fall back on – there was no paper trail. They would not issue a warranty because it was done under the table.

If the lender had gotten a sniff of the fact that there had been mold in there, we would have had no proof of remediation. Even more concerning was the fact that the mold had been removed but the cause had not been addressed. So if the mold issue cropped up again, we had nothing to fall back on.

The risks were too high (and there were signs of other places in the home where the seller had cut corners and saved money) so we walked.

Think carefully before you allow a seller to fix a problem that comes up during inspection. The vendor could hire their Uncle Joe to do the roof. If it starts leaking in six months, you have no recourse. But if you get the roof replaced yourself by hiring a reputable company, and it later starts leaking, you can chase down the company and get it fixed.

As long as what comes back from the inspector is not something that makes you want to walk away from the deal, you can use it to reduce the purchase price.

I would say that about 30-40% of the homes we have put an offer on in the last three years have had something upon inspection that has caused us either to ask for a price reduction or to walk away from the deal. *Either way, the inspection has more than paid for itself.*

REDUCE OTHER EXPENSES

Your biggest cost relates to your financing. So whatever you can do to negotiate the absolute best interest rate possible is going to save you the most money. Having an awesome mortgage broker on your team is a terrific way to do this!

Further, maximize your amortization period in order to increase your cash flow. Beyond that, simple things that reduce maintenance costs or energy costs will all save you money over the long term. While you likely won't be able to charge the utilities to your tenants if they are not currently paying for them (as per their lease); when their lease comes due or you place new tenants, put in your Lease Agreement that the tenant(s) is responsible for heat and hydro/electricity. You may have to drop your rent a tiny bit to do this, but then you no longer have to worry about expensive heating costs in the winter as your tenant will be responsible for paying them.

PUT UP A LARGER DOWN PAYMENT

If this is a great property in an area with strong fundamentals, but it won't quite cash flow with the 5% down that you've got, then look around for a bit more money. Maybe you should consider bringing in a partner who can add to the down payment? We'll talk more about this in a chapter on funding your deals. Again, financing is your most significant cost. In Canada, if you try to find a way to do a higher leverage deal, you're going to be spending a lot more on fees and rates. We find it's often better to put more money down to reduce all the other expenses you'll pay than it is to try to minimize the initial capital required to do the deal. It also reduces your risks if the market fluctuates in values.

CHAPTER SEVEN

INCREASING CASH FLOW WITH RENT TO OWN

Rent to own is when a tenant rents your property with the option to purchase it. They move in with the intention of buying it from you in the future. You set their purchase price at the beginning; they pay a fee for the option to purchase it in the future; and a portion of their rent is a credit that builds up over time towards their purchase.

It generates more cash flow because the tenants are paying a higher than market rent for their property and they are responsible for basic maintenance. You also typically don't need property management because of the quality of tenants that move in and because they are responsible for taking care of repairs up to a certain dollar amount ($300 in our case, but many other investors have their tenants handle up to $500).

The added benefit I've realized over time is that we're helping people in a really big way. Our rent to own tenants give us big warm hugs, invite us for dinner, make us handmade thank you cards – and they invest in fixing up their homes. One of our tenants painted the interior and exterior, built a garage and fenced the back yard of his home. Our regular tenants, on the other hand, rarely mow the lawn!

Typical rent to own tenants are folks who are new to Canada and haven't established credit; or they are going through a divorce and their assets are tied up; or they've beaten up their credit because of a health reason; or they haven't saved enough for a full down payment to qualify for financing; or just one setback has kicked their credit down to a point where the banks aren't interested. In all of these scenarios, they need a helping hand because the banks won't help them and the other options available don't make financial sense for them.

Most investors agree that it's a great addition to your portfolio to create more cash flow; but where the debate arises around rent to own is: What comes first – the tenant or the property?

No matter which approach you take, screening your tenants is critical. Beyond the usual tenant screening of reference checks, employment verification and credit score review, you must make sure the tenants have income levels that will allow them to qualify for financing in the future. You need to review their debt load to make sure a bank is likely to work with them in the future; and you need to review their plan to correct whatever issue they have – to make sure they know what steps they have to take to qualify for future financing. Honesty from a prospective rent to own tenant is imperative.

Where rent to own can get a bad reputation is when it's abused by investors who skip the above step. Some are lazy, some don't understand how it works, but some actually do it intentionally. They put a tenant in a home knowing the tenant will never be able to buy from them. They take the deposit and the elevated rent and when the tenant eventually cannot buy they just rent it out again – keeping all the deposits as extra profit. That's unethical and it is not how rent to own should work.

WHAT IS "PROPERTY FIRST" AND "TENANT FIRST"?

Tenant First is when you have pre-screened your tenant. They have passed your rigorous screening process, have the income and the deposit, and are ready to go house shopping. Typically, you send them out with your realtor to look for a house that they want you to buy, and your realtor has your criteria of where and what you'll buy.

The tenant finds their dream home that meets your criteria and you buy it for them. The theory is that they will be more committed to the home because they have chosen it. A lot of investors also charge a lot more to the tenant directly, such as inspection, because the home was picked by them.

Property First is when you find and buy a property and *then* find a tenant who wants to rent to own that specific property from you.

The challenge with Property First is that sometimes you don't find a tenant quickly. The reality is that the pool of people who are suited for rent to own is only a very small percentage of the rental pool. That means sometimes it can take a month or two to fill a rent to own property, and sometimes you may even find yourself turning it into a regular rental just because it wasn't attracting a tenant buyer "(tenant buyer" is what a rent to own tenant is often called).

Despite this challenge, and the fact that we have had to turn a couple of rent to own properties into rentals in the last three years because they didn't fill as fast as we'd hoped, my husband and I have decided not to do Tenant First.

We tried to do a few Tenant First deals but we found it hard to do good deals with the tenants (and their emotions) involved. The trouble is, they fall in love with a house and don't care that it's $15,000 over market price; they still want it. You can explain to them all day long that the house is a little overpriced and how about this one instead, but they don't care. And you can only say "no" to somebody a few times before they get irritated and move on. *But the reality is that if you buy a home that is overpriced at the start, you're setting your tenant up for failure!*

In order to ensure that rent to own to works as a business, you need to set a price that is above today's value. Right now we're generally appreciating our properties from today's value by no more than 4% each year.

If we pay market value (and when the tenant and their emotions are involved we find you almost always pay at least market value), do we then add closing costs and any improvements to that value? If we don't, we won't make a strong return. If we do, the price we set for our tenants to buy from us may not be feasible and the bank will not loan to that value.

To maximize the likelihood our tenant will succeed and we will make a great return, we need to buy properties for *less* than their market value. And we can't do that when a tenant is involved.

Besides – I am a real estate investor. I love helping people, but *I make money when I create a great deal.* If the tenant is the one in charge, everything unwinds from there. I am not going to buy a house that doesn't set my tenants up for success. I am also not going to buy a house that doesn't have other exit strategies or options for alternative plans.

We're coming up on four years of doing rent to owns. Our first failure happened less than a year ago. The tenants decided to move to a new city and walked from their home (and their purchase credits). When they first came to us, they wanted to do a Tenant First deal with us and they had picked out a home for us to buy. We declined to do it that way and they went into one of the homes we had available.

If they had selected their home, we'd be stuck with the home *they* had picked. The fact that they had chosen the home would not have changed their situation that led to them leaving this city!

The good news is that we bought this home $25,000 under its market value, the tenants took great care of it, and it's an in-demand property. We were very sad that they didn't follow through and buy the home; it was our first failed rent to own. When we went to fill it again, the market in Nanaimo was very soft and people were fearful about where prices would go. We tried to fill it as a rent to own for a month, but with limited interest we turned it into a rental.

Because we bought it for a good price and ran our numbers before we bought it to make sure we could carry it as a regular rental if we had to, we have options. It doesn't make massive amounts of money every month, but it brings in enough rent to cover the costs and build up a reserve fund for future expenses in the account. Again, if they had picked the home, we likely would not be able to rent it out for an amount that would allow us to cover all costs each month and still have a bit left over.

There are risks and rewards and pros and cons to both approaches, but we love to invest in real estate because of the *control* we have. Relying on someone else (the tenant) to pick the property is like giving my money to an advisor and just trusting that they're going to invest it as well as I would. I've learned that nobody loves my money like I do. My tenant certainly doesn't. When I pick the property based on location, key characteristics, and the types of homes that are more in demand by the masses (the starter family home, for instance), I set myself and my tenant up for a much higher chance of success.

CASE STUDY

To put this into perspective, let's look at how the numbers work across these two types of Rent to Owns.

PROPERTY FIRST

Purchase Price (bought for $21,000 below market value)	$309,000
Market Value	$330,000
Total Cash Required (20% down, approx. 2% closing costs, and 2 months reserve fund)	$ 70,923

Monthly Expenses (taxes, insurance)	$ 296
Monthly Mortgage Payment (80% LTPP, 4.0% interest, 30-year amortization)	$ 1,175
Total Monthly Costs	$ 1,471
Rent To Own Rent ($500 per month goes toward the Tenant Buyer's purchase credits)	$ 2,000
Net Monthly Cash Flow	$ 529
2-year Term Buyout Price for Tenant Buyer (appreciate from MV by 3.0% annually)	$350,097
Your Total Return after crediting $12,000 (+ their initial down payment) to Tenant Buyer	58.7%
Or, annual ROI to you	29.3%

As you can see, buying the property under market value by (only) $21,000 gives you an annual return on your $70,923 investment of a very nice 29.3%! Now, let's look at the numbers if you let your tenant choose the house and you buy it for them (in all likelihood at market value prices).

TENANT FIRST

Purchase Price	$330,000
Market Value	$330,000
Total Cash Required (20% down, approx. 2% closing costs, and 2 months reserve fund)	$ 75,702
Monthly Expenses (taxes, insurance)	$ 296
Monthly Mortgage Payment (80% LTPP, 4.0% interest, 30-year amortization)	$ 1,255
Total Monthly Costs	$ 1,551

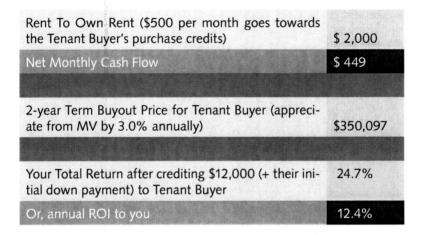

Rent To Own Rent ($500 per month goes towards the Tenant Buyer's purchase credits)	$ 2,000
Net Monthly Cash Flow	$ 449
2-year Term Buyout Price for Tenant Buyer (appreciate from MV by 3.0% annually)	$350,097
Your Total Return after crediting $12,000 (+ their initial down payment) to Tenant Buyer	24.7%
Or, annual ROI to you	12.4%

As you can see, your ROI basically gets cut in half if you buy a house chosen by your tenant and pay market value for it. It's much easier and more likely that you can buy below market value when *you* are finding (and creating) the deals.

To obtain the same return (ROI) on a Tenant First rent to own deal; using the numbers above, you have to appreciate the same property by 6.7% annually (vs. the 3.0% we used in the tables above). Is it fair to a rent to own tenant to appreciate a property by that much in a slumping or even recovering market? I don't believe so. Again, that's why we prefer the Property First approach to rent to owns.

Two final important notes: There is always some risk with a Property First: 1) you may not find a great tenant-buyer to do the rent to own with; and 2) it may take a month or two to fill it – which costs you money when the house is vacant. So, it may cost you $1,500 to $3,000 (using the numbers above) while you find a great tenant-buyer using the Property First approach; on the other hand, it would cost you almost $5,000 more in cash to buy the house at market value if you did a Tenant First approach! Carrying the property vacant for a month or two is a minor issue considering that we have multiple exit strategies when we buy using the Property First approach. Regarding #1, If we don't find a great rent to own tenant, we can rent it out as a regular rental (we only buy properties that will cash flow as *either* a rent to own or a buy and hold rental) or we can even sell it – since we bought it well below market value – to get our investment back out, even after realtor commissions. It's very tough to do any of that with the Tenant First approach.

Ultimately it's about setting our tenants up for success and ensuring our risks our mitigated while our profits are maximized.

CHAPTER EIGHT

PROPERTY RED FLAGS

OUR FIRST INVESTMENT PROPERTY

W here were you on September 11, 2001?

Dave had gone to court to represent us in the fore-closure deal that was to be our first investment property to-gether. When he came out from the proceedings, he and our realtor saw what was happening on a television outside the courthouse. I was so focused on the deal we were about to do that I hadn't heard the news until I got to the office and every-one was in my boss's office glued to his little TV.

Besides the fact that we were doing the deal amidst world tragedy, this property had gone into foreclosure and we were pretty nervous about buying it. It had sat on the market for a year before it slipped into foreclosure. We worried that we were missing the big reason why someone else hadn't bought it already. The only drawback we could see was that it was on a steep driveway. It was so steep that when it was icy, tenants had to park on the road and carefully walk up the lawn to get to the house. Not a great situation but it seemed to us that it was a property with a lot of potential.

Each side had an unfinished basement; so we could actu-ally turn it into an illegal fourplex if we wanted to. And, the property was definitely undervalued. We bought the property for $159,000 and within 12 months we had a nice positive cash flow of $300 per month. Since then, the rental rates have doubled, along with the value.

While the hill was definitely a red flag for us, the numbers on the property looked great, it met our objectives, and it's future potential for rental income growth was very appealing. We could reduce some of the issues with the hill by adding stairs, so we went for it.

Today we would not do a deal like that again. We don't like steep driveways and it did make it challenging to rent out in slower market periods. When we sold it in 2009, we caught an upswing in the market and sold it for a great price, making us over $180,000 between appreciation and mortgage pay down. It had cash flowed beautifully every month and we would have kept it, but we could see a ton of maintenance issues coming up in the next few years and we'd already made a great return on it. Sometimes it makes for diminishing returns to hold onto a property that will need lots of work in the future.

Just because we wouldn't do that deal again today doesn't make it a bad deal – we've just learned how to buy the most liquid properties and those are the same properties that attract the best tenants quickly.

The point of this story is: be aware of the things you can't control or change. We were fortunate the market was good when we wanted to sell. Had it been really soft, as it was in 2001 when we bought it, the property would have lingered on the market and we would have had to significantly reduce the price.

Getting a good deal because of an issue isn't really a good deal if that issue is always going to be there or can't be changed. *You are making an investment only if there is a reasonable probability that you will be able to make money when you sell.* Buy every property with that in mind.

Problems you can control and fix are opportunities; problems you can't control or fix are RED FLAGS!

A friend was just telling us about the people who live above him that make popcorn every night at 11:30 pm. He is in bed and he hears the WHHHIIIRRRRR sound of the popcorn maker as it warms up; then he hears the kernels drop in the bottom of the machine; and then the pop, pop, pop of the kernels as they morph into their white fluffy tastier version of themselves. Then he hears the "beep beep beep" as they put the butter in the microwave to melt it. Thankfully he can't hear them eat it. He's been putting up with this for months and he's had it; he's moving out.

When I was a renter, I had an even funnier thing happen. Darn near every night around 11 pm the couple that lived above us would get romantic. Their bed was crazy squeaky, their floor was hardwood, and there wasn't a lot of insulation between our units; so I was included in a lot more of the details than any of us wanted. I wrote them a nice note explaining how they weren't getting much privacy....

A few nights later, my roommate burst into my room at 11 pm and yelled, "Thanks a lot!" Turns out the couple had just changed rooms and were now above my roommate instead of me! We gave notice a short while after that!

If you have multiple suites in a property, do a sound test. Split up and have one person go into one unit while the other person goes into an adjacent unit. Yell, slam doors, and otherwise just be noisy. See how little (or how much) noise it takes to disturb the folks in the other unit. If a lot of noise can be heard from one unit to the next, you'll find that you will have more tenant disputes and tenant turnover. There are things you can do to reduce the sound transfer, but most options are expensive and not 100% effective.

In the older homes, noise can be a real problem. We had a triplex where you could sit in the living room on the main floor and listen to *everything* that was said in the room below. Old construction methods really didn't prevent sound transferring from floor to floor. Covering hardwood floors with carpet and a thick underlay will reduce some of the noise. But the real fix is with insulation and that is expensive.

The other culprit when it comes to noise transference is the ducts for the furnace. If it's an illegal suite, the heating will not be separate for the units, and if it's a furnace you'll find a *ton* of sound travels through the ducts.

EXTERNAL NOISE

I used to live in a small apartment by Joyce sky train station in Vancouver. People say you get used to the noise when you live by something like that, but I never really fell asleep until the train stopped running around 1:30 or 2:00am.

The property was newly constructed; the windows were double-paned; and it was as sound proof as you could get; but it was noisy and I happily moved out after six months.

Properties by a major road, or public transportation, or a fire station could all be problematic. And this noise is something that you have no control over.

COMMON ELEMENTS OR FACILITIES (CONDOS)

When we lived in Burnaby, we were looking around the Lower Mainland for investment opportunities. We came across a townhome complex in Port Moody where you could buy three-bedroom units for less than $200,000. We found a for-sale-by-owner property listing for $180,000 and the unit was rented for $1,700/month. Those numbers work really well so we had to go and see it.

When you drove into the large complex, the units were older but you could see pride of ownership. There was nice landscaping, kids playing, playgrounds, a swimming pool and recreation area. It was a fabulous place for families. The exteriors were dated but they were clean and well kept. We started to get excited.

We met the friendly owner and went inside the unit. It was gorgeous! They had finished it so nicely – there were features we wished we had in our new townhome in Burnaby. They had heated floors, pot lights in the ceiling and crown molding throughout. We were almost ready to make an offer on the spot, but I kept digging, trying to figure out what was going on. Townhomes across the street were selling for $350,000 and I couldn't figure out why there was such a big price difference between the two townhome complexes.

Bit by bit I got the story out of the owner. The complex had been horribly managed by the management company, and the bad decisions of the strata council had ruined the financial state of the strata corporation. Some windows had been replaced but there were hundreds more to do; and many decks were rotten but only some had been replaced. The maintenance list was long and there were constant disputes between the management company and the council.

The biggest issue was the fact that, rather than levy a set amount per home to just get the work done, the council voted to increase the fees because many owners couldn't afford a one-time charge of $10,000 to pay for the work. Instead of doing all the work at once, they had voted on doing it bit by bit over time – dragging it out and making it way more expensive. The fees were high and were only going to go higher and higher. With the current council in place, the issue was never going to be resolved, and the current council showed no signs of going anywhere. It was a mess. Once you factored in all the extra fees and potential levies that could be coming, you would lose money on the property.

The seller actually admitted they were selling both their units in the complex because they anticipated more costs and ongoing problems. I pulled the strata minutes to see if it was as bad as she said it was (all the minutes were conveniently located on a website for the complex) and walked away without looking back.

A well managed condo or strata building can be a great

investment because much of the maintenance is handled for you. The issue is that you have *no* control over the fees or the decisions that get made unless you're sitting on council. If you're thinking of buying a condo, make sure you research the condo history and the strata minutes and look into the finances of the corporation.

PARKING

Extra parking can be an opportunity. In Alberta, a lot of investors rent out separate garages for as much as $200/month. That's great added income without much added expense! We didn't have a car when we lived in a condo in Toronto so we rented our space to another resident in the building who had two cars for $800/year.

The opposite is also true. Lack of parking for a property reduces your potential tenant pool, lowers your cash flow, and increases tenant turnover. The triplex we used to own in Toronto had an old run-down garage. One car could fit in there, but in the winter when the snow piled on the caving roof, nobody wanted to even consider parking inside for fear they'd wake up one morning with the garage roof on top of their car.

With three two-bedroom units in this property, we usually had at least six people living there. The property is really close to a subway stop and less than 1 km from the University of Toronto, so while many tenants didn't own vehicles, there were usually at least two vehicles owned by tenants, *plus* visitors. Whenever we filled vacant units, parking was always one of the questions potential tenants asked about. Street parking was limited to two hours unless you had a permit; the city charged for the permits and many tenants didn't want the hassle of getting a city permit.

One day we decided we had to deal with this issue. Dave and his buddies had a big "manly destruction party" and pulled the old garage down, and then we hired a company to build a modular carport in its place. The new carport did several things: it created two appealing parking spaces that we could now charge $50/month for, and over time that amount could be increased because it was an appealing option compared to street parking.

STORAGE

Similar to parking, if you don't have any place for your tenants to store their belongings (think golf clubs, bikes, skis, snowboards), they will be unhappy. And you don't want those items stored inside your unit because they will cause a lot of wear and tear. Also, if you have extra storage, it can be rented out for additional income.

And it's not just about renters. The lack of parking or storage will impact your resale value.

DESIGN AND LAYOUT

Design often comes down to personal preference, but there are layouts that have good flow and ones that don't. When you walk in a home and it has a good feel, it's often because of an open layout. The layout allows for good light flow and easy, functional living. Bad flow makes you feel cramped or constrained, and it often makes a place seem dark and out of sorts. You will usually just know it when you see it. What is more difficult is to know WHY you feel that way and whether you can easily fix it.

First, it's critical to understand what is a good flow for a property. Usually it's instinctive, so it's tricky to explain; but things you can watch for, i.e., things you don't want, are:

- A bathroom that exits into a dining area – unless it tucks away nicely, it's kind of weird.
- Bedrooms at the entrance – bedrooms should be tucked away from the noise of the home.
- Rooms that lead into other rooms – rather than to a hallway.

- Large wide hallways or thin narrow ones.
- Kitchens that seem too squished or too vast.
- Random walls that block light and don't serve a purpose.

If you're not sure whether a property has a good flow or not, and you don't feel like you understand this, speak with a few people who might be able to explain some key elements to you. Good realtors will understand a lot of this, but interior designers and home stagers can explain a lot of these concepts really well.

NEIGHBOURS

To everyone that drove by, the old character home in the Old City Quarter of Nanaimo was hard on the eyes. People probably had dreams about burning it down; it was that ugly. We didn't see it the way most people saw it. Few people could see beyond the grey and dingy stucco with flaking purple trim, or the sheds covered in graffiti and filled with dead rats, garbage and crack paraphernalia. And physically it was impossible to see beyond the overgrown yard, full of junk and bushes that hadn't been touched in at least a decade.

We bought it and tackled a massive renovation job, investing $70,000 into improving the property – including full exterior and significant interior improvements. People all over the city acknowledged the change we'd made and how much better that corner now looked.

During the renovation, we caused a small amount of damage to our neighbour's rock wall that was effectively the property line between her place and ours.

When the accident happened, we apologized immediately and gave her all our contact information. We assured her that we would pay for the repairs and we offered to get the wall fixed, letting her know that we had a team of people more than capable of doing an excellent repair job. But she refused; she wanted to use her guy. We agreed and asked for the name of the person that she wanted to use to repair it, saying we would take care of the bills.

She refused. She wanted to be the one that coordinated it all. She wanted it done right and she felt we'd be inconveniencing her if we communicated with her contractor. We weren't really sure how that would be the case, but we let her handle it the way she wanted.

The wall was completely redone a week later – much better than it was before – and we received an email from her saying only: *The work is done. You owe me $645.73.*

Dave responded with: *"Please send me an invoice as I cannot just pay you a random amount without a receipt. Please have the invoice include an amount for labor, materials and taxes, as this is what I require for my tax purposes."*

We didn't hear anything for a while and wondered what had happened. Then weeks later she sent us a nasty email saying that her contractor was going to be away for two months so she couldn't get the invoice until he got back. She went on to say that she and her family were experiencing financial hardship because she had gone ahead and paid him and now we weren't paying her.

Had she allowed us to work with him directly, this never would have been an issue, so we felt so frustrated. She was making us feel like horrible people, yet she was the one that was being difficult to deal with.

A month later I was showing the property to a prospective tenant when the neighbour knocked on the door. My first reaction was to hide, but I knew that was pointless and somewhat juvenile.

I took a deep breath and opened the door. She launched at me verbally: "You're Dave's wife, right? Can I come in?"

I said, "I'm busy with some people at the moment."

She ignored me and tried to push by me to come into the house. I certainly didn't want the tenants to know the neighbour was bat shit crazy, so I stepped outside with her and closed the door behind me.

She was looking at me with fire and fear in her eyes. "When do you plan to pay me? We're suffering because you guys aren't living up to our agreement."

I calmly said "We have never once said we won't pay; we'll pay you once we receive the invoice. Send us the invoice and we'll pay you."

She said "When?? When? When will you pay me?"

I tried to stay calm but I hate confrontation. And I really hate the feeling I get when someone doesn't like me. I felt like crying but I didn't. She wanted to know how we would pay and where we would put it. She showed me specifically where she wanted the cheque placed and then she left.

As soon as we received the invoice from her, we dropped of the payment and we haven't heard from her again, but we live in fear that we will.

We dread what could happen in the future should we need to do further renovations; or worse, if we decide to develop that property (we bought it because of its future development potential). We keep hoping a FOR SALE sign will go up at her house.

That's really a minor incident, so imagine how much bad neighbours could impact you and your tenants' lives. You will experience lots of tenant turnover and complaints if you have bad neighbours beside your properties. One good idea is to visit your potential purchases at 11pm as well as at 5am and 2pm to get a really good sense of what is going on in the area and with the neighbours. Of course new neighbours can always move in, but you don't have to *start* with bad ones!

RENTAL SITUATION IN THE AREA

When you do your location research, you will look at the vacancy rates for a city. And you will look at the direction that rate is trending. But you should also take a look at the area you are buying in; take a four-square-block area and look at the rental situation. How many rentals are there within your area?

Is there a handful within a four-block area or are there dozens? Again, if there are a *lot,* find out why. If there appears to be an excess supply and not enough demand, you may want to reconsider buying in that area. High supply and low demand means lower rent and thus less cash flow. So know your area for house prices *and* rent rates.

I mentioned earlier that we bought a beautiful duplex unit in Kelowna, BC in 2009. It's just steps from the lake, shopping and lots of recreation. But the rents have decreased almost every year. Right when we bought it, the condo market tanked and developers had to rent out their units because they couldn't sell them.

We should have paid closer attention to the impact all the unsold product was about to have on our rent rates. Things are improving now, as the units have slowly been absorbed into the market and the overall market is gaining some strength again, but we've been feeding that property a bit every year to carry it. Overall we're making money, and our partners are still earning a return because of mortgage pay down and small appreciation rates each year – but our rental rates have been a challenge.

CHAPTER NINE

LET'S MAKE A DEAL

Many people will claim that you just need to know their winning strategy and you'll be the deal-making dude or diva of your decade. What they aren't telling you is that their strategy will work once in a while but that there isn't any strategy that works every time. Each deal will require a slightly different approach. Many people in the education space won't tell you this, because if they admit that there are many ways to do a deal, how can they tell you that they have "THE" winning strategy?

Sometimes a strategy works and other times it will scare someone off completely. *But the big thing to remember is: you can analyze a deal to death but until you make an offer you'll never really know what you're dealing with.*

At the point where you're ready to make an offer, you know what you want to get from the deal. You know you like the market that this property is in, and your initial evaluation tells you it's going to be close to neutral cash flow or positive cash flow each month so long as:

- You can buy it for the price you want to pay;
- The expenses are not more than you've estimated;
- The rent is what you've estimated it to be, or higher;
- The property doesn't need any major repairs; and

- You can get the terms you would like (this may be related to vendor take back financing, bank financing, or even a particular closing date).

Until you make an offer on a property and get it accepted, the information you need to find out about these last details will likely not be available to you. So go ahead and make your offer; just *make it subject to at least one condition* so you can get out of the deal if things don't check out!

While you should always approach every offer with the intent of doing the deal – you also want to ensure you have a period of time to do due diligence so you have a way out of the deal if something comes up that doesn't make the deal look so good anymore.

SO WHAT DO YOU PUT IN AN OFFER TO PURCHASE?

The Offer to Purchase (also called Purchase and Sale Agreement) is a binding contract. If this is your first purchase, sit down with your real estate lawyer to review the contract so you understand what you are signing before you send it over to the vendors.

A real estate agent may be able to explain the clauses to you, but if you aren't sure, it's *always* best to consult the services of an attorney.

We are not lawyers. This section is merely to provide you with a *basic* understanding of an Offer to Purchase, but you need to consult your own legal counsel for advice.

Your offer must clearly define what you're buying, the terms under which you are buying it, and at what price. If you are working with a realtor, make sure that you are in charge – not them. *You* determine what you are offering – not them.

Many of our coaching clients have come back to us after asking for a VTB (a vendor take back mortgage, which is where you're asking the seller to carry some or all of the financing – I'll explain this more when we're talking about funding your deals), or when they have put a small deposit on their deal, but their realtor says they can't do that. We have a high amount of appreciation and respect for our realtors, but many times they try to guide us to put things in our offer because that is how it's "normally" done, not because it *has* to be done that way.

Here are some important things to understand:

PARTIES TO THE CONTRACT

The contract will need to show who is the vendor (seller) and who is the purchaser. If two people own the property, make sure both people are on the contract. As the purchaser of the property, you'll want to give yourself as much flexibility as you can with regard to who will ultimately be on the title of the property when you close on it.

The primary reason we include the additional flexibility in the deal is because we will usually be doing the deal with a joint venture partner who will typically be on the title. We haven't talked about this yet but we will.... How the heck can we buy $3,000,000 worth of property in a year without using much of our own cash? We use other people's money! I'll explain this in the next two chapters.

But the thing is, when we're making the offer, we don't always know who that partner will be (in fact we never make an offer in someone else's name unless we're working on a foreclosure and it's going to go to court. In that case we do work with a partner who will be making the offer). Otherwise, it's too much of a pain to go back and forth with our partner to get signatures for every step in the negotiation; so we make the offer in our name, negotiate it out, and when the offer is finally accepted we amend the contract with our JV partner's name or company.

One thing that used to be taught by many real estate courses was to put in the offer as "Dave Peniuk and Julie Broad and/ or assigns."

We used to use this type of wording all the time, but it's not widely accepted anymore. In fact, I think the real estate boards in some areas do not allow it at all because people were using it to wiggle out of a deal. What we do now is include a subject in the deal which allows us to change the name on the contract without absolving us of our responsibility to close on the deal.

Discuss this with your lawyer, but in most cases you actually have the right to assign the contract even if you don't have the "and/or assigns" clause in there. The important point is that you are legally bound to fulfill the deal, so if your assignee doesn't complete the deal you will be responsible for doing so.

NOTE FOR COUPLES

We don't *both* go on title for any of the deals that are done under our name, unless it's necessary for financing reasons. There are a lot of reasons we do this but the two big ones are: it makes it simpler (less documents required) and it means that only one of us is getting a hard check on our credit. Remember that when a bank or some other company checks your credit with a hard check (versus a soft check which is like a landlord looking at a tenant's credit score), you can be deducted points for credit seeking.

If one of you is not working or has bad credit, there are additional reasons to consider not going on title together. In Canada there are also first-time home-buyer advantages and other considerations that may give you a good reason to not both be on title. We highly recommend you ask an accountant and a lawyer about your specific situation so you can make the best decision.

ADDRESS

Make sure the contract states *what* you are buying. This should be the street address as well as the legal description. A legal description usually includes a lot number, block number, and district number, as well as the municipal area (your realtor, or the seller, or your lawyer will have this information).

TOTAL PURCHASE PRICE

You agree *who* is buying *what* (the property obviously, but it could also include some furniture or appliances) from *whom*, at *what price.*

DATES

You will have a couple of very important dates on your offer to purchase. You will have today's date ... the date of the offer. And there will be a date that this offer expires. We usually give our vendors 12 hours. If we know they are away or not available, we give them 24 hours max. If you leave it open too long, then other competing offers can come in, or they can shop it around letting others know they already have an offer.

There will also be a date by which any conditions you put on the property have to be removed or else the deal falls apart. Usually you will want to ask for *at least* five business days for a financing and inspection clause; we almost always ask for 10 business days. Sometimes sellers try to negotiate this, but unless you're making offers in a hot market, 10 business days is pretty reasonable. In a hot market, you'll want to be more aggressive in order to compete and have a smaller number of days for removing your subjects.

DEPOSIT

This is a "show of good faith" to the seller that you are serious about your offer. Usually we will give $1,500 with the offer (to be held In Trust either by either the realtor's agency or our lawyer). If the sellers aren't happy with this amount, what we usually do is offer another $3,000 to $5,000 in addition to the $1,500, but only once we remove all conditions we've put on the property. The deposits are put toward your down payment on the property if you go ahead with the deal.

Realtors often push us for larger deposit amounts suggesting that it shows we're serious. If that happens to you, politely explain that you're a real estate investor, and you're making more than one offer this week, and you don't want a bunch of money tied up on a bunch of different properties. They will usually let you have it your way. On the occasions where we have walked from the deals, it has taken up to three weeks for the deposit to be returned to us. That makes us extra hesitant to tie up more than a few thousand dollars until we're sure we're going forward with the deal and are ready to lift conditions.

There is *no rule* that you have to give a 5% deposit once the deal is accepted, although some agents have tried to tell us there is.

The most important point to make with regard to a deposit is that you should *never* give the vendor your deposit directly. And it should never be made out to the vendor. You will usually make this out to the realtor's company "In Trust." If you aren't using realtors, you can make it out to your lawyer "In Trust." Provide the seller with proof, from your lawyer, that they have the funds.

> Note: you will often hear people refer to "subjects" and "conditions" interchangeably. A contract is **subject to** certain **conditions**. When they are asking about the date that subjects are to be removed, they are referring to the conditions of sale.

If you decide not to buy the property, and you do not lift the conditions by the specified date, then your total deposit will be returned to you.

But, if you remove all your conditions, and then change your mind at the last minute before completing the purchase, you will lose your deposit. You could also be sued. That is why it is so important to complete *all* of your due diligence before removing your conditions.

CONDITIONS, OR SUBJECT TO'S

Most of the conditions of sale will come from the vendor (especially in the case of buying new construction properties, but that is an entire book on its own). But you, as the purchaser, should include at least one condition to your purchase so that you have time to finish your due diligence before being committed to the purchase.

We usually include two conditions. The first is that the offer is "subject to getting financing that is satisfactory to the buyer." This allows you to waive conditions, or walk away from the deal, if you can't get financing that works for you.

And we usually make our deals "subject to a property inspection." As part of this condition, the vendor must make the property available to our property inspector within enough time for them to inspect the property and get us the report before the conditions must be waived.

If the property currently has leases in place with tenants, you may also wish to make the deal conditional on seeing all of the leases for the current tenants. Or, subject to a review of any of the condo condition reports (or condo meeting minutes). Or, subject to proof of any major renovation work that the vendor says has been done (new roof, new wiring, or something else that is not as obvious to the naked eye; for example, new carpet, or new trees being planted in the front yard). You can also ask for *vacant possession* if the property is occupied by tenants but you don't want to keep the tenants in place (although this may not be allowed depending on the state or provincial residential tenancy laws where your property is located, so you'll have to check your local regulations before you ask for this).

ELEMENTS OF A CONTRACT

You've probably heard of deals done "on the back of a napkin." While I would always recommend you involve a lawyer, contracts done in unconventional ways can be legally binding.

Basically, for a contract to be binding it needs to have five elements:

1. It needs to be entered into with mutual agreement.
   • The terms of the agreement need to be specific, complete and clear and the people involved in the agreement must be easy to identify.
2. Any parties to the contract must have the legal capacity to enter into the binding contract.
   • In most places this means they must be the age of majority, or able to vote.
   • They cannot be under the influence of any drugs or alcohol.
   • They must not be medically insane or under duress of any kind.
3. Something of value must be exchanged. This is called "consideration" because that something of value does not always have to be money. It could be a promise to do something in the future in exchange for the property, or a service of value in exchange for the property.
4. The contractual parties must intend to form a binding contract.
5. The contract must be for something legal in nature. In other words a contract between a drug dealer and a drug seller for the price of their drugs would not be upheld in a court of law because it involves a contractual agreement to do something that is not legal.

MAKING THE OFFER TO PURCHASE

IMPORTANT TERMS AND CONDITIONS TO INCLUDE

If you've taken any no-money-down real estate investing courses – as we have – you may think that the offer to purchase is a time for playing games to manipulate the seller into giving you the best price and the exact terms you want.

One of the strategies we learned in the courses we took was to include many conditions, sometimes over 10, in the original Purchase Agreement. Supposedly by including so many, you empower the seller by allowing them to strike off a few of them. This starts the negotiation process – seller strikes off 1 or 2, then you strike off 1 or 2, then seller strikes off 1 or 2, etc. This gives the seller the "feeling" they are winning some points because they are getting you to remove conditions – when in fact you didn't care about them anyway! In our experience, it is *not* necessary to play this game.

Good real estate agents are not going to go along with such a strategy, and a private seller is going to freak right out if you try to do that. You look unreasonable when you throw in eight additional clauses to the contract – and it's not necessary. If you've done a good job understanding what problems you can solve with your offer, all you *really* need is *one conditional clause* that will allow you to walk away from the deal if your due diligence turns up something that is not good.

If you've found a property with a relatively motivated seller, then put in your conditions (usually subject to financing and subject to an inspection) and don't allow the vendor to remove them.

If the property is currently tenanted, make sure the Purchase and Sale Agreement includes the following condition (or a condition similar to this as recommended to you by your lawyer):

- Subject to the Purchaser's review and approval of all documents related to the tenants in the property, including leases, income and expense statements, pre-occupancy inspections reports, etc.

If the property is owner occupied or vacant, make sure the Purchase and Sale Agreement includes the following condition (or a condition similar to this as recommended to you by your lawyer):

- Subject to the Purchaser's review and approval of all expense documents related to the property, including all recent utility bills, tax assessment, and any major repair or renovation-related bills, etc.

It also is advisable to have what is called a "hold back" if there is a lot of junk on the property. Our former real estate agent told us about a property that a new agent in her office sold. The yard was full of old cars, car parts and household junk. When the buyers arrived on closing day, all of the junk was still in the yard. The deal was done and the sellers were long gone. They buyers had to spend nearly $5,000 getting rid of all the junk in the yard. Had the real estate agent acting on behalf of the buyers had enough experience, she would have known to put into the contract a hold back that would have $5,000 (or some other set amount) put into an account held in trust by the lawyers, so that if the property, upon possession, was not free of all the junk, the buyers would at least have the money required to remove the junk.

If you're negotiating on a property filled with someone else's crap that you do not want, make sure you include such a stipulation so that the sellers either clear it up or you're compensated for having to do so.

In almost all purchases, you should have a professional inspection done of the property. A Condition like the following one should be used:

- Subject to the Purchaser's review and approval of a Property Inspection to be completed within 10 business days upon acceptance of this offer.

Stick to simplicity, and you'll find the buying process is much easier and more efficient. You don't want to be going back and forth and back and forth on condition removals. Besides, a confused mind says no!

TERMS TO CONSIDER INCLUDING

There are also some Terms that you may want to include in your Purchase Agreement. Terms are not binding like conditions – whereby a breach of a condition means you (or the Seller) can get out of the offer; rather, they are components of the Purchase Agreement that must be adhered to. Here are two Terms you may consider:

- The Seller agrees to allow the Purchaser to show the property to prospective tenants in private, with 24 hours' notice given to the Seller.
- The Seller agrees to allow the Purchaser and/or its contractor access to the property, with 24 hours' notice given to the Seller, to complete any inspection or estimate costs.

With these terms in place, if the seller does not provide you with access in either of the above terms, you could sue the seller for damages. They may wish to limit the number of times you can access the property before closing on it. In that case, you (or the seller) may want to include the number of times you can have access to the property, which is what we typically do in our offers, as you will see.

CLOSING DATE

One final important item to consider (and include in your offer) is the Closing Date.

The Closing Date is when you actually close on the deal and own your investment property. In many instances, it's recommended to close at the beginning of the month. The reason is because by closing on, for example, the 3rd of the month, you have the remainder of the month to complete any renovations, clean up the property, or show the property to prospective tenants who may be able to move in at the start of the following month. And, because your first mortgage payment usually commences approximately one month after you take possession of the property, this gives you a bit of breathing room to get new tenants in place and collect their security deposit (or last month's rent) and their first month's rent once they move in. Further, if there is already a tenant in place, if you close at the beginning of the month, you will get a credit towards that month's rent. It will be pro-rated for the number of days within that month that you now own the property.

The Closing Date could be a LARGE negotiating point with the seller, so make sure you find out how important it is to them! Some of our best deals have been because we were able to give the sellers the exact Closing Date they needed (and in exchange we get a price discount or some other term that is favourable to us).

Often, if you've found a *vacant* property, you will get a better price the faster you can close on the property. Or, if there is a family living in the property, you may be better off allowing them to tell you when the best date to close is, again in order to minimize the price you pay for the property.

LAWYER SELECTION

When we went to that "Get Rich Quick" course we've talked about, one of the things they recommended early on in the first weekend was to make sure we had two lawyers on our team. First, we needed to hire a cheap lawyer to do our real estate contracts. Second, we needed to hire a high powered lawyer who could go to court and be a ferocious tiger when we needed one.

At the time, this sounded exciting and smart.

Looking back, I realize it's *totally insane*. What kind of investment deals are you getting into if you need a ferocious tiger to defend you?!

Even with all of the problems we experienced with the manslaughter, crack house and fire code violations, we didn't need a ferocious tiger lawyer, or even a high powered court lawyer.

My personal preference is to focus on risk mitigation, and thereby minimize the likelihood that you'll ever need a high-priced courtroom attorney!

On the other hand, it's essential to have a good lawyer advising you. It's also helpful to have a lawyer in each province or state that you purchase in, because local laws affecting real estate will be different in each area.

NOTES ABOUT YOUR POWER TEAM

Some of the real estate training out there says that when you want to become a real estate investor, the first thing you need to do is build your power team.

I've heard a lot of "would be" investors say they are "not ready to buy a property because they haven't yet put their power team together."

Having a good lawyer, property inspector, realtor, mortgage broker and accountant on your side is important. But if you are brand new to real estate investing, and you are hung up on finding and building your power team before you've even purchased a property, you are focused on the wrong thing.

Your team will come and go and frequently change. Some people leave their industry for something else, or leave the area for other prospects. Our top real estate agent – it took us seven agents and several years to find our perfect agent – up and left us to become a West Jet flight attendant. Our electrician went to Afghanistan for a high paying job. On the other hand, we outgrew our accountant and needed a more sophisticated one. And the list goes on! We're over eleven years into the business and we're still building our team. Find the people you need when you need them and always be on the lookout for new team members!

OPTIONS FOR NEGOTIATIONS

It's not just about the price!!!

In Toronto, during the hot housing days in 2003 – 2005, we had many friends that were desperate to buy a house. And what one of our friends did was start approaching the vendors with an emotional appeal. Some of the houses were being sold by seniors that had lived in their home for 50 years. They'd raised their kids in that home and had entertained their grandchildren in that home. As they proceeded to move on into a retirement home, the most important thing to them was NOT always money.

At that time, a normal starter home in a good area of Toronto would go on the market for $550,000, and then it would sell for $700,000 in a heated bidding war. In situations like that, the offer that was the highest with no conditions often won. Our friends were getting desperate after losing out on nearly 12 different bids. When they came upon this gem of a house in Bloor Street Village, steps from Bloor Street and close to two subway stops, they knew they'd found their house. Two sisters had lived in the home for nearly 40 years. The rugs had never been changed and the walls were covered in ancient wallpaper. The kitchen cupboards were nearly antiques. And it was ugly. But the lot was abnormally deep and our friends knew they could easily expand their house later on and still have a nice backyard! (And that is exactly what they did, by the way!)

Our friends went in with an offer that had no conditions on it, and they offered over the asking price, but only up to their budget; they knew they couldn't pay a dime more. They also knew that the sellers wanted all of the appliances to stay with the house so they put that in their offer. But they did something else to help them get the deal they wanted.

They wrote a lovely card to the sellers explaining that they had been married for three years and were ready to start their family. They explained that when they saw their beautiful home they could see how happy their children would be there, and they knew that it would be a safe and warm place to raise their family. They included a wedding picture so the ladies would know who they were. Sure, they stretched the truth a bit in saying they wanted to keep the home just as it was … but the essence of the home did remain the same. The crusty carpets and wallpaper had to go – and a few years later they did redo the kitchen and add on to the home.

But the bottom line is that they appealed to the emotions of these two senior ladies and they got the house. They know for certain that their offer was at least $20,000 less than two other offers, but the ladies wanted the two of them to have the house. The ladies loved the thought of their house being full of children and a loving family. And they were comforted to know that their house was not going to be ripped down and rebuilt.

Today they have added on to the home; they put about $150,000 into renovations and now have a place that is probably worth $1,300,000. More importantly to them, they have a home they love and it is filled with their two active boys!

Never assume. Always ask questions and find out as much as you can about the sellers and about what they want out of the deal. Think win/win; or even better, think of how you can make the pie you're splitting bigger.

Most people come into a negotiation thinking the pie that is to be divided is a certain size. Instead, try and come into a negotiation and think about ways to make the pie bigger. Negotiations that seem fair may still not be the best deal for either of you because you didn't really spend the time figuring out what was important for you or for the other party.

HOW CAN YOU MAKE A BIGGER PIE?

So, other than price, what are some ways to expand the pie in a real estate deal? Here are some ideas, and you may be able to think of others.

1. *Including or excluding things like appliances and other chattels.* Remember, a chattel is anything that isn't built into the property, like furniture, window coverings and appliances. We know people who have gotten cars thrown

into the deal. When my mom and dad bought their lake-front home in Nanaimo in 2012, my Dad got the sellers to throw in their boat. He was thrilled, but later wished he'd asked for their boat trailer as well!

2. *Closing date:* Years ago when Dave's sister and her husband were shopping for a new home, they found one they loved. It was vacant, so Dave suggested she offer a super quick closing with the deal. Sellers of vacant properties are spending money every month for something they aren't using and they appreciate quick sales. But his sister thought only about the hassles of moving so quickly and decided they needed more time. Her offer lost out to a competing bid that had a quick close date!

3. *Terms and Conditions:* We were negotiating on a property that was being sold by the deceased's estate. Specifically, the estate was the former owner's two sisters. The home was full of the belongings of their brother – and I do mean full. He had lived there since he bought the home with his wife in the 70's. The sisters lived far away, so we offered to get rid of anything they didn't want to keep as part of the contract. We wanted to buy the property for a great price and get the closing date we needed, so we were willing to do other things to make it easier for them. We could take the time selling the stuff online or giving it away to local charities; it wouldn't cost us much but it saved them a lot of time and hassle. As a result, we got the property for a great price and they didn't have to spend a lot of time dealing with furniture, books and other belongings from afar. And, in fact, we were able to give away almost everything left in the house so our disposal costs were minimal. We simply put an ad on Kijiji saying that at 9 a.m. we'd be putting filing cabinets, shelves and other household items on the curb – free to anyone that picked them up. By 9:20 a.m. everything was gone.

4. *Seller Financing:* If you obtain seller financing, sometimes it allows you to offer a higher price for the property. The

seller gets more money and a monthly cash flow, and you get a property without going through the hassles and time of getting bank financing. It also may allow you to buy a property that you can't get financing for at all.

There are plenty of other potential things you can do to increase the size of the pie, but really you won't know until you understand the situation of the seller. Spend a bit of time learning the reason for the sale, and if you can, meet the vendors. Get to the bottom of what they really want. And, remember, it may not be what they are saying.

Always remember that a good negotiator is a good problem solver. A good problem solver can only be good if they actually know what problems they are trying to solve!

THE 10 COMMANDMENTS OF NEGOTIATING REAL ESTATE DEALS

1) DO BETTER THAN YOUR ALTERNATIVES.

I once heard Keith Cunningham, author of *Keys to the Vault*, say that the only reason you are in a negotiation is to do better than your alternatives – so, make that your focus instead of "winning."

This happens all the time on the Canadian television show *Dragon's Den*. On one episode, a guy selling a rice alternative initially turned down an offer for 50% of his business in exchange for expertise and cash that he badly needed. He admitted that if he didn't get a deal, his only remaining option was to move on from the product, yet he almost said no because he felt 50% was too high. He was seriously considering being the not-so-proud 100% owner of a $100,000 loss instead of accepting the opportunity to have 50% of a $5,000,000 a year business. Thankfully he came to his senses and grabbed the deal before it was yanked off the table; but for a moment, he'd lost site of the fact that he was there to do better than his alternatives, not look like the king of negotiations on Canadian national television.

2) BE A PROBLEM SOLVER.

Why is the person selling? Ask lots of questions to try and understand the seller's motivation. Then figure out how you can offer the best solution to their problem. We bought a property a few years ago for about $25,000 under its market value at the time because we asked questions and found out that the sellers were building a new home. They needed to know their home was sold so they could finance building their new home; but they were unable to firmly commit to a move-out date until the home was further along. We gave them a flexible close and got a great price in exchange.

Many times the sellers are moving provinces or cities due to a job relocation. They may be under a real time pressure to sell but won't tell you unless you ask some clever questions to find out.

In most cases, what you want to find is someone who has a problem they need solved more than they need their full asking price. But we also look for people who maybe want the best price for their property but they are willing to make other concessions for us (like offer us seller financing or the ability to bring a lot of people through to get estimates for a renovation).

Generally people will not just *tell you* what you need to know to figure out how you can best help them. You'll have to look around the property to find signs and ask good questions to get as much information as you can.

You won't know what kind of deal you can create unless you focus on *solving the problem of the seller.*

3) PICK A RANGE AND STICK TO IT.

Before you begin a negotiation, determine what is a good deal for *you*. And this will be a *range*, not a specific number. If you get any number within your range, take the deal. Resist the urge to squeeze for that last $2,000.

4) REMEMBER, IT'S NOT JUST ABOUT PRICE WHEN YOU'RE NEGOTIATING A GREAT REAL ESTATE DEAL.

You'll often find that you can get the deal done with less hassle and fewer expenses if the seller will finance the property. In that case, it may be worth it to pay more than you were originally willing to pay. Alternatively, the seller might throw in furniture, vehicles, art work or even some services (dentistry, massage therapy, auto mechanics ... etc.) just to get a higher price on the property.

5) BE FLEXIBLE WITHOUT BEING EMOTIONAL.

The purchase price range is a good thing to have, but you may choose to bend it if you find other ways to make the deal work for everyone. Maybe the sellers need their cash but they don't want to move for a year. You could rent it back to them afterwards and delay renovation costs, for example.

The trick is to be able to analyze the deal without getting emotional. If at any time you start to feel yourself getting too emotional, take a step back. Review the numbers and the facts of the deal. What makes this a good deal for you?

This is also where you might like to have an experienced third party opinion. We've helped some of our coaching clients create great deals (and save $14,000!) by providing that third party, *unemotional*, unbiased opinion.

6) OPTIONS = POWER.

When you think about what your options are, you realize that there *will* be other deals; and no matter how much you like this property, it's never worthwhile to overpay for a property just to get it.

We always remind ourselves and our clients that we *never* need to buy as much as someone needs to sell; and if it starts to feel different than that, it's time to walk away.

One question you can always ask yourself if you start feeling like you *want* to do this deal: If I don't reach this agreement what will I do?

7) OPTIONS = POWER FOR THE SELLER TOO!

Give your seller choices. You have a better chance of understanding their problem and getting the deal you want if you make the seller feel like they have some power and control over the deal.

For example, to avoid having the seller say "no" to my offer, I would say something like this: "The best I can do is $200,000 if I have to go to a bank for financing. They're going to require me to prove the rental income, pay for an appraisal, and do a ton of paperwork to qualify for that loan. So if you'll accept my $200,000 offer, I will close on the date you want. But if you are willing to provide at least 70 percent of the financing, I can offer you $210,000. And I would still be willing to close on the date you want."

By giving my seller these two options, I make him feel like he is in control of the outcome of our negotiation … even though either one would be a great deal for me.

8) A CONFUSED MIND SAYS NO.

When have you ever been confused and agreed to do something? It just doesn't happen.

Explain your offer so simply that an 8-year-old would understand it. And if you're relying on your realtor to tell the seller's realtor, and then the seller's realtor to explain it to the seller, consider writing a letter to be presented with the offer – just to make sure the seller gets the simple explanation.

9) EXPLAIN WHY.

In Robert Cialdini's book, *The Psychology of Influence and Persuasion*, he explains the details of an interesting study he did on *the power of why*. He determined that even a poor reason why is far more influential than no reason at all. He references a study by a Harvard social psychologist, Ellen Langer, who studied *the power of why* in a line-up of people waiting to make copies. When someone asked to go to the front of the line most people turned them down. When they said, "Excuse me, I have five pages; may I use the Xerox machine?" 60% of the people allowed the test subject to go ahead of them (which is shocking in itself because everyone was in line to make copies). When the same question was asked with the addition of "because I am in a hurry," 93% people let that person go ahead of them!

So when you're making an offer, be sure to provide a reason for the offer. Explain the rationale behind why you're offering less than market value and why you need a certain time frame. You don't have to show all your cards, but you should give the seller every opportunity to accept your deal.

10) NEGOTIATING IS NOT A GAME; NOR IS IT A SPORT.

A negotiation is not something to be won. It's something that cannot be judged by win or lose, but by results. In fact, I would argue that it's more of a science or an art. It's something that is very individual, but it's also something with principles that are fundamental to every negotiation. Do *not* let your negotiating become a game or a sport, and you'll find that you are less likely to try to be *right*, which means you are much more likely to be *rich*!

In every real estate deal, you'll have a desired outcome. If you keep the above principles in mind, you'll remember that you have choices and that you only do deals that make sense for you and your goals.

A negotiation is simply an opportunity to do better than your alternatives. If you have good alternatives, then you'll make a great deal – because you have options, and options give you power!

CHAPTER TEN

GETTING THE MONEY

D espite some gory stories of property managers robbing rent money from us, fire code violations, tenants being taken away by police, and a property manager charged with manslaughter; I don't regret many decisions we've made in our eleven years of real estate investing. We are excellent investors today because of all we have learned.

The main regret both my husband Dave and I have is that we didn't try harder to finance more deals while we had jobs.

Even with four years of running our real estate investment business full time, eleven years of never missing a mortgage payment on any property, and a substantial net worth, we still find it challenging to finance our investments.

We bought a triplex that cash flowed beautifully in 2012 and the banks required us to have three years of mortgage and interest payments just hanging out collecting dust in a bank account. That was on top of the 25% down payment that also had to be sitting in a bank account for 30 days before we could even apply for the mortgage.

We paid $325,000 for the triplex. In order to even *apply* for the mortgage we had to have about $130,000 in cash just sitting around.

If you have a job now and are thinking of leaving it in the future to start a real estate business, I encourage you to finance as many properties as you can while you have what the bank perceives to be *a secure job.*

You'll also want to start planning for your funding and financing future. Eventually the banks will say no to your next property purchase – even if you have a good job – or you'll run out of the funds to do the deals you want to do. It's nothing to worry about because there are plenty of ways to do deals where you aren't the one that has to have the money or the bank financing! But it's a good idea to start planning for that *now.* It took us about 12 months of full time effort to get to a point where we could fund any deal we wanted to do with other people's money. We did deals in the meantime, but it was heavy lifting to raise the money. Today we have a list of happy investors waiting for the next opportunity, but when we didn't have that, deal making was sometimes exhausting.

Here are some important things you need to know about getting the money for your deals – whether you have a job or not!

GETTING A MORTGAGE BROKER WORKING WITH YOU

Many real estate courses recommend building relationships with bank managers. They tell you to create a binder or a packaged portfolio of your current investments and write a business plan. Then you're supposed to sit down with each banker, explain what you are doing with your investments, and sell yourself and your plan.

Well, in our experience, the banker who is going to take time to talk to you has no more authority to lend money to you than if you went online and applied. It's a nice idea, but it doesn't work very well. Even if you do happen to find a good banker that wants to work with you, this will likely only work for you on property 1 and 2. Good bankers get promoted, relocated, or just leave the bank; and your efforts to build that relationship will all be for nothing. Relying on one person within a bank to determine your financial future is not a good idea; it certainly hasn't worked for us.

Where a good bank relationship can make a *difference* is when you *also* own and operate a local business. We have one joint venture partner who has done five deals with us, and we have found that the best rates and programs available to finance each property were through the bank where she does her business banking. But that is an exception, not the rule.

We have two mortgage brokers. Our main guy works for one lending institution, understands our business and works hard to present our deals in a way that gets us the most favourable rates and programs available within his institution. We have a second mortgage broker – a more traditional one – that will shop a deal around to a bunch of lenders.

Both are a very important part of our team to ensure we get the best rates and access to a variety of programs.

WE TURN TO A MORTGAGE BROKER BECAUSE:

- Banks usually pay the fees, so their service is often at no cost to you, unless you are buying commercial property (in which case you will usually pay the bank a fee).
- Mortgage brokers have neutral opinions on your financing options.
- Brokers can more easily find the best rate for you from a long list of lenders, as they have already built relationships with many lenders and have systems to quickly send a mortgage application out to a bunch of lenders all at once.
- They will perform one credit check, and this one credit check will be submitted to any lenders they seek financing from on your behalf. (This prevents multiple checks, which can decrease your credit rating.)
- Typically they can obtain financing for you no matter where in the country you live. (So you can maintain that relationship if you move or if they move).

- They will prepare your portfolio for you (this is especially helpful and time saving for you if you own many properties, as the banks require a package of property summaries and analysis).
- High volume brokers will get even lower mortgage rates from certain institutions, providing the opportunity for you to benefit from their volume.

Our last few purchases and refinances (where it's just been my husband Dave and/or myself on title and on financing) have been challenging. Without the hard work of our mortgage broker, we don't believe we would have been able to obtain financing in time to remove conditions (and thus, keep the properties).

FINDING A BROKER

Ask potential brokers the following types of questions to find a good fit with your personality and your objectives.

- Do you typically work with property investors?
- Have you done many deals with investors?
- Do you have preferred rates with particular lenders?
- How long have you been working as a mortgage broker?
- How many deals do you typically do per month?
- Do you have any investment properties yourself?
- Do you charge any fees or are you paid directly (and only) by the lender?
- Are you familiar with the Rental Cash Flow Analysis using the 1.1 Debt Coverage Ratio? (This can be a way to obtain financing once you have three or more rental properties.)

Once you find a mortgage broker that you want to work with, you'll typically be asked to fill out an application form; and then you have to give the broker all the documents he or she needs. This includes a copy of the contract to purchase the property, proof of employment or proof of income, and potentially a bank statement showing where the down payment for the property currently is. You will likely need a letter from your employer, or if you're self-employed you may be asked to show the last two to three years of financial statements from your business.

Your mortgage broker will then order an appraisal of the property (which you will typically pay for) and run your credit score. *Note:* property appraisals are not always required by lenders, but you need to be aware that this could be an additional cost to you. We always ask our broker to cover the cost of the appraisal or have them push that cost back to the lender.

MORTGAGE BROKER SERVICES

Most mortgage brokers will offer two types of service. One, as described above, is where the mortgage broker is paid a commission or a referral fee from the lender. In this case, you don't pay any money out of your pocket for the broker's service.

The second service, which most brokers will offer in addition to the above, is when the broker works on complex mortgages that he will shop to lenders who either do not pay them a commission or are not traditional lenders. Typically these lenders have private money and will hold second positions, offer secondary financing, or give more flexible terms than a traditional lender will. But typically you will pay them a fee, and you will also have to pay your broker a fee or a commission for the work he does to get this financing for you – because he won't get paid directly from the lender.

It's good to build a working relationship with a mortgage broker that can offer both types of services. That way, even if it costs you a bit more money to get financing on the hard deals, you can almost always get the money you need for your investment.

Detailed numbers bore me; and I tortured myself by forcing myself to get an MBA in finance and real estate – I thought I needed to strengthen my weaknesses. I *should* have been taking marketing or communications – things I love and excel at!

That's a lesson for another book. The bottom line is that I wasn't smart enough to realize in school what areas I was weak in; but I must have known it, at least subconsciously, when I got married because I married a man who *loves* numbers. After working as a mortgage broker for five years, Dave is a key resource for our business and for our clients when it comes to analysis and financing.

And you can thank him for all of the following information!

There are so many elements that determine how much you can qualify for in terms of a mortgage. Your credit score, your provable income, your net worth, your liabilities, the property you are financing, the location of the property, the city and province and state, and even the country, are all factors that play a role in your financing. Because of this, we can't tell you exactly what you may or may not qualify for. But we can give you an example or two to help you understand the main elements that lenders use to determine the level of financing you qualify for.

STEP 1: YOUR GROSS INCOME

The Lender will want to verify your annual Gross Income. If you work full-time and are salaried, this is pretty simple to verify (through paystubs, employment letter, etc.). If you work part-time or you're self-employed, you'll need to show two or three years of income tax statements. Basically, whatever you sent to the government for paying income tax is what you'll need here.

STEP 2: MONTHLY EXPENSES AND PAYMENTS

The Lender will want to find out all the monthly payments

you have to pay. This includes any lines of credit, bank loans, student loans, mortgages, credit card payments, car loans, etc. – anything that you owe and must pay a minimum payment on every month. The lender will tally these up to calculate your total monthly expenses.

STEP 3: DETERMINE YOUR GDS
(GROSS DEBT SERVICE OR MORTGAGE TO INCOME) RATIO

This formula is mostly utilized on your residence and/or first or second investment property. Once you own three or more investment properties, a different ratio – Debt Coverage Ratio (DCR) – is often used. Your mortgage broker can explain it in detail, but essentially it's a way of calculating the amount of cash available in your portfolio to service debt payments. For now, let's focus on the GDS formula, which is:

GDS =
monthly mortgage payment (principal and interest) +
property taxes + heat
divided by your monthly gross income (before taxes)

EXAMPLE GDS (OR MORTGAGE TO INCOME) RATIO:

Gross Annual Income =
$45,000 (divide this by 12 to get monthly = $3,750
Monthly Property Expenses =
Mortgage Payment on prospective property = $1,050
Property Taxes = $180
Heat (if the landlord has to pay it, as opposed to the tenant) =
$75
Total GDS Payments = $1,305 ($1,050 + $180 + $75)

$$GDS = \frac{\$1,050 + \$180 + \$75 = \$1,305}{\$3,750} = 34.8\%$$

So, your GDS in this instance = 34.8%

Is this good or bad? Well, the standard rule of thumb is that the maximum a lender will want is around 32% GDS. In the U.S., this is sometimes a bit higher, and if your credit score is really strong (680 or more), the lender may waive this criteria and only use the TDS ratio.

STEP 4: DETERMINE YOUR TDS
(TOTAL DEBT SERVICE OR DEBT TO INCOME) RATIO

Let's look at that ratio:

TDS =
total monthly debt service payments
your monthly gross income (before taxes)

Thus, using our example again, we found the following:

Gross Annual Income =
$45,000 (divide this by 12 to get monthly = $3,750

We now have to include ALL other monthly obligations. Here's an example:

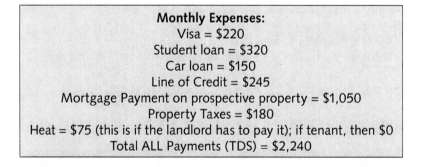

Monthly Expenses:
Visa = $220
Student loan = $320
Car loan = $150
Line of Credit = $245
Mortgage Payment on prospective property = $1,050
Property Taxes = $180
Heat = $75 (this is if the landlord has to pay it); if tenant, then $0
Total ALL Payments (TDS) = $2,240

TDS =
$2,240 = 59.7%
$3,750

In the US, the TDS is often referred to as the **Total Debt to Income** ratio; and as in Canada, lenders prefer to see it no more than 40-45%. At this point, we urge you to get familiar with a mortgage broker or your banker to better understand how these ratios are calculated in your city and with your prospective lenders.

In the above example, while the GDS (or Mortgage to Income ratio) is just a little high at 34.8%, it's important to note that the TDS (or Total Debt to Income ratio) is *much* too high! The good news is there are a few things an investor could do to bring this percentage lower. For instance:

- If the tenant pays the heating bills, the $75 can be removed from the calculation.
- If you have the cash, you could pay off some of the monthly payments, again to remove that value from the calculation.
- If it's going to be a rental property, you can add approximately 50% of the monthly rental income to your income, thus increasing your total income, and thereby decreasing the TDS ratio.

Let's take a look at the numbers if you are able to implement the above suggestions:

Pay off your Visa balance (bringing your Visa payment to $0); determine that the tenant has to pay for the heat (remove $75); and determine that there is a current tenant in place renting the property for $2,000 per month. Most lenders will allow you to add approximately 50% of that rent to your income (thus, add $1,000 to your income). Now, let's look at the ratio:

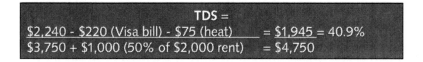

$$\text{TDS} = \frac{\$2,240 - \$220 \text{ (Visa bill)} - \$75 \text{ (heat)}}{\$3,750 + \$1,000 \text{ (50\% of \$2,000 rent)}} = \frac{\$1,945}{\$4,750} = 40.9\%$$

Now, that's more like it! And while a 40.9% TDS (Total Debt to Income) ratio is a bit high, many lenders will be okay with it as long as you can verify your income, debts, and rent.

NO MONEY DOWN – NO BANK NEEDED

If you watch late night infomercials, you'll probably feel some attraction to the *no money down, no qualifying at the bank* strategies.

We've invested almost $40,000 into learning the *no money down and no bank needed* investment strategies. The first time we went down that road I was in school – so not only did I not have a job; I also didn't have any money at all. I was living on loans. The second time was after the bank rules changed in 2009 and we were self-employed (aka, not financeable in the eyes of most banks).

We learned a few lessons that I'd like to share with you now. The biggest lesson is: **Just because you can do deals with no money down doesn't mean you won't need money.**

For example, in some real estate courses, <u>sandwich leases</u> are often put forward as a good way to do *no money down and no bank needed* type deals in Canada. A sandwich lease is simply where you find someone who will allow you to lease option their home from them; and you turn around and offer it as a rent to own to someone else. You pocket the difference in monthly cash flow and the option fee from the tenant.

In theory, this is a great strategy to do deals without money or banks. The reality isn't as pretty. It takes a lot of marketing effort (and potential cost) to find the deals. It also takes a lot of effort to educate and explain to the seller what you're doing with their property. You'll also find the houses are generally in a state of disrepair and need some investment to improve them so you can attract good rent to own tenants. How much money do you want to put into a house you don't own?

The final issue is aligning your lease option term with the timeframe within which your rent to own tenants are able to buy. It's tricky. It's a very hard business to be in, and you'll find very few people successfully close on more than one or two sandwich leases in their entire real estate career – no matter how hard they try.

Besides sandwich leases, there are other creative strategies that don't require banks – like wrap mortgages and agreements for sale; but what we've learned from doing these types of deals is that they aren't the ones that allow you to live the life you're dreaming of.

Real estate is a way for us to create location and time freedom. We always expected to work for the money, but we wanted to be able to *work when we wanted to and wherever we wanted to.*

We found that when we did "creative" deals, we ended up with problem properties and challenging tenants. In other words, we basically created *a full time babysitting job* for ourselves. The kind of deals you can do "creatively" are generally not the good properties in good areas. They don't attract the best caliber of tenant and they don't have minimal maintenance requirements.

The creative *no money down and no bank needed* strategies can work, but for us they weren't an effective way to create the life and business we wanted.

However, there are still a lot of options available to help you build a great portfolio without YOU needing the cash or the approval of the bank.

- The strategies we use to fund and finance our deals include:
- Vendor Take Back Mortgages (VTB's),
- Private Money,
- RRSP mortgages, and
- Joint Venture Partners.

Sometimes we use a combination and other times we use just one. These strategies allow us to focus on doing great deals in areas that attract the best tenants. Our tenants typically love their homes as if they were their own, apologize when they are late with rent or give us a heads up that it might happen, and rarely call us with problems. These strategies allow us to focus on doing the deals that allow us to create a business and life we love, instead of doing deals just because we can do them with little money down or no banks.

VENDOR TAKE BACK MORTGAGES

One simple way to solve your financing challenge is by simply asking this question of every seller: *Will you carry financing?*

Not every seller is going to say yes; in fact most will say no. But you won't know unless you ask!

Seller financing, more commonly called a VTB or vendor take back mortgage, is simply where the seller (vendor) of a property is willing to provide some (or all) of the mortgage financing on that property.

Seller financing can take several different forms. We've done deals where the seller provided the entire mortgage, which amounted to 80% of the property value. For example, we paid one seller 6% interest amortized over 25 years for a 3-year term, with no prepayment penalties and an option to renew. She was able to sell her house in a slower market and make more money from it with a VTB because we paid her interest for 3 years. When we paid her out at the end of the three-year term, the total of what she earned from the transaction was thousands more than her asking price.

We also have used seller financing to top up traditional bank financing. In other words, we've had sellers provide us with a second mortgage (which simply means they are in second position behind the banks) to minimize the money we had to put into a deal. We've also used it to bring the financing on a property up to 80% of the loan to value when a bank would only loan 65%.

In hot housing markets, it can be hard to find sellers willing to entertain financing as an option. However, with cooler housing conditions taking over across most cities in Canada, we're finding more sellers willing to entertain the option of financing some (or all) of the property to increase their return, speed up the sale, and get a good price for their property.

Private money is simply money from an individual. It's different than hard money. Hard money lenders finance deals for real estate investors as a business. They are more sophisticated in their investment terms and will typically seek quick repayment at high interest rates. With private money, you can have more control over the terms of the loan. You can offer terms that suit your needs and offer a good return for your private lender.

The easiest way to find private money is to call your favorite mortgage broker and ask if they have any private lenders. Most mortgage brokers work with a few wealthy folks that have money to lend. If you have decent credit and the property generates a solid cash flow, you should be able to find money this way – but that money is fairly expensive.

The upfront fees on those funds are usually 1-3% of your mortgage amount. On a $250,000 mortgage, for example, that means you can start off with a $7,500 fee, and then pay at least 7-8% (or more) interest on the loan. That's okay if you're in a pinch with a strong cash flowing property, but our preferred source of private money is to raise it ourselves.

We find that a lot of folks have paid off their homes and are willing to put a line of credit on the property and loan that money out for a premium. We've borrowed $330,000 on someone's line of credit to buy and renovate a property. We paid them 5% plus their line of credit costs (with no upfront fees). In another deal, we pulled together two private lenders for over $200,000 and we paid them 7% with no upfront fee on an 80% loan to value property.

With GICs and savings accounts making less than 2%, it's

actually fairly easy to find people with cash they are willing to loan out for a great return backed by a cash flowing asset. You'll find these folks everywhere from someone at your kids' swimming lessons to your next door neighbour to your chiropractor. It's just a matter of knowing how to ask.

RRSP MORTGAGES

Mutual funds and stocks are not the only investments that are RRSP eligible. A mortgage can be held in a self-directed RRSP (or RESP, LIRA, or RRIF) account. This is probably the largest untapped source of funds available to real estate investors because very few people know this option exists.

Master this and you'll always be able to find the funds for your deals. With no management fees or advisor commissions to pay, RRSP holders can make a stable and predictable 6%, 7%, or even 10% or more return on their money inside their RRSP.

When holding a debt obligation in your RRSP; you have a lot more control over the risk, you have a say in the return you get, and you actually have recourse if you aren't making the return you were promised. (Ask your Mutual Fund or Stock Advisor what recourse you have if those funds go down in value or disappear altogether.)

There are, however, some additional rules around using RRSP funds. For example, you cannot borrow funds from your immediate family (spouse, sister, parents, etc.) to fund your investments. It needs to be arms length. You also can't use RRSP funds for a down payment directly on that same property you're borrowing against. You'll need to secure the RRSP funds on one property as a first or second mortgage and then use those funds as the down payment on the new investment property. Or you can use your own down payment funds, and then the RRSP funds from your arms length private lender can hold the mortgage on that property (with no bank needed!).

(We learned how to do RRSP mortgages by reading Greg Habstritt's book *The RRSP Secret*.)

JOINT VENTURE PARTNERS

This is the most powerful strategy in our investment tool box. It's the strategy that has allowed us to comfortably add a new property to our portfolio almost every month.

Our joint venture deals typically are structured so that we find the deals, oversee all the work and management, and split the proceeds 50%/50% with our partner. In exchange for all our experience, expertise and efforts, our partner puts in the cash required to close on the property and puts their name on title so they qualify for financing from the bank.

If anything goes wrong with the property and requires cash, we are partners and we split the costs 50- 50 just like we split the positive cash flow and profits.

Busy people love this option. They don't want to spend the hundreds of hours we've spent learning an area, building a team and digging up deals. And they definitely don't want to take calls from tenants or handle issues around the property management. They can get into real estate without the hassles of being a landlord.

For us, it allows us to continuously grow our portfolio and net worth, increase our cash flow, and do it without requiring us to have hundreds of thousands of dollars sitting in our bank accounts just to make the bank feel comfortable

Each one of the strategies discussed above could be an entire book unto itself. In fact, the perfect follow-up book to this one would probably be one entitled *What Nobody Will Tell You About Getting Money for Your Deals.*

There are a lot of inauthentic, greasy or high risk strategies being taught all over North America for doing deals with no money or without your own money. Our way of raising money may not be sexy but it's a natural and effective way to do it. It works to find partners with $70,000 and private lenders with $500,000, and any other amount below or above that.

CAUTION: THE FRIENDS AND FAMILY TRAP

Some very influential people in the Canadian real estate space teach a course and have a book on doing joint venture deals. The core of their strategy is to raise money from friends and family. They rightfully argue that it's the *fastest and easiest* source of money because the people who know you the best are the ones most likely to trust you with their money.

It's true that it may sometimes be the fastest and easiest source, but it's much more complicated than that. After soliciting friends and family members to work with us on a number of deals, we were left with a really crappy feeling. Many of the people we love and cherish actually ignored us when we asked to speak with them about our deals, and others turned us down. Plus we felt that some of our friends and family purposely distanced themselves from us after we talked to them about possibly working with us.

Friends and family may sometimes be the easiest source of funds, but there can be a massive emotional price to pay – even if everything goes well. And when something goes wrong with your deals, the stress, strain and guilt you will feel can cripple you.

I met an investor recently who had paid this price but didn't even realize it. We were talking about his biggest real estate business challenge; and he said it was overcoming the lack of funds to do more deals. He shared this story, saying: "It took me three years to convince my sister and brother-in-law to work with me, but now we're joint venture partners on three deals."

He was proud of the accomplishment. He had three investment properties and he'd used other people's money. But he was clearly struggling to continue. He wanted to buy more property but he was still faced with the challenge of raising money; he was frustrated that nobody else would invest with him when he'd already done three successful deals with joint venture partners.

The piece he didn't see was that his success had only been with immediate family members, and even though he didn't know it, the fact that it took him three years to bring his own family on board was taking a toll on his confidence. *If you aren't confident in what you can do and what you have to offer, you will not be able to raise money.* I don't think he was even aware of the price he was paying.

In my opinion, one of the worst things you can do to yourself, your family and even close friends is raise money from them. If you have a strong relationship with someone outside of a business environment then the relationship will change if you try to work with them on a deal.

One of our most cherished friendships is with a friend who partnered with us on a deal in 2009. We were new friends at that time but over the years we've gotten closer and closer. The deal we did with him is so far the worst performing deal we've done with a joint venture partner. We're not losing money on the deal but it's had some financial challenges. It hasn't been anywhere near as profitable as we'd expected (right now it's about an 5% per year return on investment vs. the 15% we expected, and it's not generating enough cash flow to cover all its annual costs). His money is still doing better in this property than it would be just about anywhere else he would have placed it; however, we feel horrible that we haven't done better for him. In a few cases, we have chosen to not make cash calls when we had to do renovations because of the guilt we feel about having to ask him for money on a deal that shouldn't have needed more cash to feed it each year. If we didn't have a close friendship with him, we would not feel that guilt and would treat it like the business transaction it is, and ask for the money required.

The reality is that when you try to raise money from people you love and who love you, you'll find that one of three things happens, and each one comes with a *gigantic* emotional price:

1. They don't want to say no and hurt your feelings, so they avoid you or avoid the subject, and your relationship becomes awkward and strained.

2. They say *yes,* but only because they want to help you and support you. Subconsciously (or consciously), you *know* they are investing with you because of your relationship, and it plays enormously on your confidence and your ability to raise money outside of the family.
3. They say *no,* and you feel hurt. "Why don't they trust me? Why don't they believe in me?"

Then there's the other part of the picture. The price you will pay if something goes *wrong* with the deal can be monumental. Here's a story that an investor shared with me on the condition that he remain anonymous:

Once upon a time there were two brothers. These two brothers brought their big families together every year for major holidays. All 40+ family members would pile into a warm, love-and-laughter-filled house to celebrate the season and each other.

This happened for many years until a real estate deal the two brothers did together turned bad and suddenly they couldn't stand to be in the same room together. Now the entire family is torn apart and there are no festive get-togethers anymore.

This is not my story, but it is a true story. The investor that generously shared this story with me in the hopes that others could learn from his situation said: "Looking back on it, when we first got into REI, I was blinded with the excitement of getting into the game, and I really didn't step back and figure out whether my values and goals matched up with those of my family members. I really wish I would have figured that out sooner, because I found out that my idea of an acceptable rental property was not their idea of an ideal rental, and the way I handled tenant-landlord issues was also different. So I always found myself defending my decisions … and at the end of the day I felt like an employee, not a partner. So I really had no choice but to leave."

He was so sad and regretful, and he obviously wished he had never mixed family and real estate.

Recently I met someone else who had a bad experience. He had brought his parents into a deal four years ago and it had cost his parents an unstated sum of money when the deal ended up totally falling apart. All the money they invested in the deal vanished. The money was definitely a big loss, but he made it clear that the real cost was the guilt that weighed heavily on him every single day.

I am not saying he wouldn't have felt guilty if he'd lost someone else's money; but I am suggesting that the guilt he feels over his parents is far greater because he knows they invested in *him* more than the deal.

Investing with family members can potentially be rewarding when things go well, but there are a lot of areas where things can go bad. I think it's critical to be realistic about how solid the deal is and to ask yourself if it's worth risking damaging your family (or friend) relationships.

Having said all that, sometimes family situations can work out. My husband Dave and I have been investing together since September of 2001. His first deal, though, was in 1993 with his Mom. He never would have gotten into real estate at such a young age (19) if it weren't for his mom's passion for property.

As for my parents, they are active commercial real estate investors in Alberta and have been for 30 years. For Dave and me, they have acted as private lenders for small amounts of money at various times in the past, and they have provided invaluable advice. After years of working together in smaller ways and realizing there was an opportunity to grow together, my mom and dad and I and my husband Dave formed a family corporation in 2009. They invested money and a huge amount of time into ramping up our business to the point we're at now. They've since stepped away from active duty as they are fully into their retirement but they are still in the corporation for now.

I don't regret the decision to join forces with them, but it hasn't been without its bumps. For me, the biggest issue is that when I stop in at Mom and Dad's for a visit on a day off it can turn into an impromptu business meeting. Sometimes I leave their house feeling stressed, even though I was relaxed when I walked in. The lines between personal and business become blurred and that is a big issue for me.

It's just not easy when you mix family or close friends and money. To increase the likelihood of success, here are some very important things to protect your relationships *and* your financial interests – and these are also things that other investors I spoke with suggested as ways of ensuring a harmonious and prosperous working relationship with relatives.

Before you even get into a business relationship – whether it is a loan, a partnership or a corporation – with any of your close family members, consider the following:

1. IS THERE REALLY A GOOD FIT? IS EVERYONE BRINGING SOMETHING OF VALUE TO THE TABLE? WHAT IS MOST IMPORTANT TO EACH PERSON, AND GIVEN THOSE CONSIDERATIONS, IS THERE ALIGNMENT?

A lot of times the *only* reason you're lending money/borrowing money or working with someone is *because they are a family member.* That is absolutely the *wrong* reason. Philip McKernan (author of two best-selling real estate books and personal growth coach) suggests that borrowing money from close family is not a good idea because they can never clearly evaluate the deal or the risks. They are blinded because of their close relationship to you.

There's a lot of truth to that. Ask yourself and those you are considering working with if bloodlines are the only reason you're getting into business together.

If you are going to work together, there has to be a fit. If there is no fit, there is no long term compatibility, but rather a giant pothole of potential problems.

Have an open discussion about risks, problems and the kind of deals you're expecting to do. If you aren't on the same page about what kind of deals you want to do, and how you're going to do them, and the kind of tenants you want to work with; it could be a horror story. These types of differences mean you'll always be butting heads and constantly working harder than you need to.

2. DISCUSS ROLES AND RESPONSIBILITIES – THEN PUT THEM IN WRITING.

This is one of the challenges we have faced with our corporation. When we first started, my mom and dad provided our new corporation with some short term loans at low interest rates. Dad was handling nearly 1,000 calls from potential seller leads; my mom was overseeing renovations; and Dave and I did everything else around negotiating, managing, and raising money for the deals. After a year or so, Mom and Dad started getting tired of working so much and were not interested in putting more money into the company – short term or otherwise.

That left Dave and I to fund anything that the company couldn't fund itself *and* do all the work. Even though we knew this would be the case when we started the corporation, Dave had some hard feelings about this for a while. It could have festered and become a big issue, but we had a corporate meeting and revised our roles, responsibilities and compensation levels.

In any company, roles, responsibilities and compensation have to be clear and fair or there can be hard feelings. With a family business, it is no different.

3. TREAT THE BUSINESS RELATIONSHIP LIKE A BUSINESS RELATIONSHIP.

It's very common to go easy on a son or daughter, or even

a parent, when you know their personal struggles. It's also possible that you might take advantage of the fact that someone knows your struggles and use this as an excuse to not live up to a commitment you have made. *But in business a commitment is a commitment – and it has to be the same when it involves family.*

One investor I know put $20,000 of his own money into a few troublesome properties because he didn't want to make a cash call to his family members. He put *massive* financial strain on his wife in order to save face with his parents and siblings.

This stemmed from the fact that the core of the family/business relationship was an emotional one, not a business one. If these were non-family investors who evaluated the deal on its business merits versus investing in the deal because it was their brother or son, the cash call would have been easier.

4. CREATE WORK/HOME BOUNDARIES.

One of my biggest pet peeves regarding getting into business with family and even friends is that social get-togethers become impromptu business meetings. I live, work and play with my business partner so it can be *really* hard to separate work and home. That gets exponentially more difficult when we visit with my parents. We try to set the boundaries so we know when a lunch is a meeting versus a family catch-up time. We create agendas for our meetings and try to ensure that get-togethers aren't impromptu business meetings. It doesn't always work out as nice and neatly as I would like; but with the boundaries stated, I don't feel rude when I say I just want to visit with my parents and not have a shareholder meeting.

5. COMMUNICATION IS CRITICAL; ASSUMING IS DEADLY.

This could be an entire book and it probably is somewhere; but the big thing is that you can't assume that you *know* what someone is thinking just because you've known them all your life. Ask for each person's point of view and listen. Watch for nonverbal cues that someone is holding back and be prepared to push for honesty. Be as quick to express positive results and outcomes as you might be to point out issues and challenges. Finally, focus on one issue at a time; and make sure expectations and plans are clearly articulated before moving on to the next issue. Write everything down for even better results.

Creating a successful business requires all of the above factors, regardless of who your partners are. It just becomes a different situation when you're working with family members because of the blood ties and the lifelong relationships you have.

It can be fun to work with your family, and it can be satisfying to come together and successfully create something. But there can also be enormous challenges if you aren't partnering with the right folks for the right reasons. Hopefully you're now ready to take a step back and make your decisions carefully.

5 TIPS FOR CREATING AUTHORITY AND CREDIBILITY AS A REAL ESTATE INVESTOR

Police officers, EMTs, sheriffs, security guards, and doctors and nurses have uniforms they wear to work. Have you ever considered the importance of their uniform? When one of these professionals walks into a room wearing their uniform, it creates instant authority and credibility. People who have never met them before give them their attention and even their trust. But without the uniform, they may not command the same respect and authority.

As a real estate investor, your business depends on your authority and credibility. The level of success you'll find as you interact with sellers, tenants, buyers, lenders, joint venture partners, real estate agents and other people you do business with depends on their trust in you.

The challenge we all face as real estate investors is that there isn't a lab coat or magical jacket you can wear to create that authority and credibility.

There are, however, things you can do to create more instant credibility, such as:

- Dress appropriately for each situation. What you'll wear to meet with a plumber or a bricklayer may be different than what you'll wear to meet with a joint venture partner or a lender, but in every case you want to look clean cut and professional.
- Do what you say you're going to do: this is as simple as showing up or calling when you say you're going to show up or call.
- Be upfront about your situation: Ditch any tacky sales and negotiation techniques you might have learned that involve trying to trick people into doing what you want them to do. If you have an agenda, most people will know – and they will definitely know if you are not being honest about it – so just be truthful about what you need from the situation.

These simple credibility tips will go a long way when you do a transaction with a realtor, mortgage broker, seller, buyer or tenant. They will even help with joint venture partners and private lenders, but you'll find this surface level credibility isn't quite enough to grow and expand your business much beyond a handful of properties if you're using other people's money to expand.

When you're asking someone to invest their $200,000 RRSP savings into a mortgage, or you're looking for someone to invest $70,000 for the down payment on an investment deal, the returns you're offering will only be a small factor in the minds of the JV partner or lender. Your credibility and authority will be their main concern.

Keith Cunningham, business mentor and author of *Keys to the Vault,* says "Money follows management." If you're looking to have the money follow you into your deals, you need to demonstrate that you, as the manager of those funds, are capable and trustworthy.

A track record of success helps, of course, but there are other things you can do to establish yourself as an authority to be trusted. Creating authority and credibility takes work; but once you make the effort to do this, you'll typically find yourself in a position where growing your real estate business gets easier. For example, the money for deals *will find you,* instead of you having to go out and find the money.

CREDIBILITY CREATOR #1: BECOME AN AREA EXPERT

I know – you're probably saying "Not this again!"

I wouldn't keep talking about it if it wasn't a game changer.

What's worth more to you – someone who is a generalist or someone who is a specialist? Sometimes you need a generalist to point you in the direction of a specialist, but in almost every example I can think of, from doctors to car mechanics to computer programmers, the more specialized the person is, the more money you will pay for their services. It's the same for real estate investors.

Real estate is a very *local* business. The exact same house can be worth $20,000 more one street over – simply because of an ocean view or some other desirable feature. If you don't know a market well, you might miss that and buy the house *without* the view or the desirable feature for more than you should, just because the nearby properties make it seem like that's what it's worth.

In our case, our particular focus adds authority and credibility because we can confidently say what a house should sell for, what its best qualities are, what it will rent for, and what the primary risks are with a house in that area. We can speak knowledgeably about the sales activity, the schools, the employment, the development, and what the city has going on in our target areas. We know who to speak to in the City offices for most issues and who to call when something unexpected arises. We actually have employees of the City of Nanaimo who frequently read and respond to our weekly revnyou.com newsletters because we've become known for our local investment activity.

We have a lot of local joint venture partners that choose to invest with us rather than trying to do it on their own because of the fact that we have such deep and intense expertise in the area. They see tremendous value in working with us rather than investing the time and energy to develop that level of expertise themselves.

CREDIBILITY CREATOR #2: CREATE A MEDIA BUZZ

Press releases are an underutilized tool by most real estate investors in Canada, yet a story that has local appeal, market relevance and a great angle can create a lot of media buzz. When my husband was awarded *Canadian Real Estate Magazine*'s Reader's Choice Award for Best Real Estate Investor, we issued a little press release in the local market. Dave had the "local boy gets national recognition" angle, plus the story was amplified by a Re/Max report that had just come out with a gloomy forecast for the housing market for the year.

The local angle plus the market relevance made for great news. He was interviewed for a local news broadcast, written about in three newspaper articles and two local magazine articles, and then invited for additional interviews and feature pieces. All this publicity from one press release resulted in multiple prospective joint venture partners calling us, an existing JV partner stepping forward for another deal, and plenty of fun conversations with family and friends that had seen Dave in the local media.

CREDIBILITY CREATOR #3: GET SOCIAL ON SOCIAL MEDIA

Dave gets his Canucks hockey updates through a Twitter stream on their official website. He says the updates are great for staying up-to-date on a game when he doesn't have time to watch it. So Twitter is useful for sport updates, but many people think social media is a waste of time for business. If you're one of those people, you're probably not using it right.

Through Twitter and Facebook, I've made connections with people all over North America. When I am in a bind for a tradesperson or a cleaning lady, or I need help with a problem, a quick Tweet or a post on Facebook can often yield the contact or the answer I need. Even more significant, some of those connections have developed into business partnerships, business deals, and even a few close friendships. But none of those came overnight.

Creating a presence on social media takes time, effort and persistence – much like successful real estate investing. If you're up for it, the keys to creating positive and productive relationships from social media are:

- Be yourself! Don't try to be what you think people expect you to be; if you do, you won't make real connections.
- Add value to others. Focus on helping and supporting other people, as opposed to only thinking of your own agenda.
- Reach out to others. Create conversations. If you use Twitter, take a look at how many times you've replied to others, versus how many times you've just talked about your deals, your articles or your life. Make it a point

to interact with others *more* than you talk about yourself. The same goes for Facebook. Comment on others' thoughts and posts.

- Here's the money maker: once you've established some online relationships, take them offline! Have phone conversations or meet up at "Tweet Ups" or other local events. During the Winter Olympics in Vancouver, I turned many of my Twitter contacts into friends by meeting them at various pavilions around town. When I went to Florida, I had dinner with a Facebook friend and then we became business partners for a while! Start the relationship online and take it offline. Then watch your credibility and authority sky rocket!

CREDIBILITY CREATOR #4: BLOG ABOUT REAL ESTATE

Just writing a newsletter or a blog doesn't give you instant credibility; but over time, as you establish a presence, grow your audience, and consistently share more stories and lessons, your credibility can grow exponentially.

My husband and I have been writing a real estate investing newsletter for almost seven years. Many of our JV partners spend a lot of time getting to know us online before they decide to trust their hard-earned cash to us.

That's *part* of the credibility boost, but a *larger* part of the credibility and authority comes from the impression others have that "we are everywhere."

Dave's uncle in Seattle was trying to find a renovation tip video on YouTube recently and told Dave's Mom, "I kept seeing Julie's renovation videos – she's everywhere on YouTube." We started with a newsletter, then built a website, and eventually added videos and speaking engagements. Today we have almost 150 videos on YouTube, and I've written hundreds of articles for online and offline sites all over North America. Some have a readership as small as a few thousand but a couple of the publications I've been published in boast half a million readers. Both Dave and I have spoken on the stages of major real estate events all over Canada from Vancouver to Halifax and many cities in between. Not only do we share great content through *our own* publications; we've also grown our presence through other channels. In exchange for the ideas, stories and lessons that we share, we get links back to our website and the borrowed credibility of being featured as experts.

Over time, this approach has enabled us to grow our online presence at a low cost, cemented our expertise as real estate investors, and created a lot of authority and credibility for us in the eyes of JV partners and private lenders.

CREDIBILITY CREATOR #5:
SUPPORT YOUR LOCAL REAL ESTATE CLUB MEETINGS

One of our coaching clients was struggling to get a JV partner. He and his wife were diligently attending darn near every real estate meeting they could find in BC's Lower Mainland for months. It wasn't until he stepped up and was the speaker at a meeting that everything changed.

He gave a talk on rent to owns – and boom! – he had a partner and a deal within a month, as well as several other potential partners. He and his wife believe so strongly in the value of a good local real estate club that they decided to start their own in Surrey, BC. (http://www.meetup.com/SurreyREIC/)

Crystal, another one of our coaching clients made $45,000 on a flip in Victoria, BC. She found out about the property through a local real estate club member who didn't have the time to tackle the project. If she hadn't been active in the club, she would never have known about this deal that was in pre-foreclosure.

For years we didn't attend any real estate club meetings. Some early experiences with guru real estate courses and club meetings run by people with questionable intentions scared us away from club meetings for many years. And then both my husband and I were busy building careers in the real estate space and we didn't have any interest in adding club meetings to our schedule.

When we left our jobs and became full time real estate investors, all of that changed. We were hungry to find colleagues doing what we were doing; and we no longer had coworkers to commiserate with so we had to find a community.

At our first local club meeting four years ago, I somehow found myself volunteering to speak at the next meeting. I just wanted to share some of our experiences and support some of the others in the room. The organizer of the club didn't know me but he thought I seemed knowledgeable and credible so he agreed to have me out at the next meeting. Little did I know that I was about to uncover the ultimate source for credibility and authority creation: active involvement in your local real estate investment club!

After my first speaking engagement, we found that being involved in local club meetings resulted in tremendous opportunities in the form of private money, joint venture partners and even deals. In 2010, we had two partners, three private lenders and one deal all come to us as a result of being active in the club meetings!

Attending is a step in the right direction, but it is not enough to develop credibility and authority. You need to stand out from the crowd and let your expertise shine! Speak up when there is an opportunity to introduce yourself and share what you're working on. Go out for drinks afterwards with some of the other members to get to know them better. And do whatever you can to support your club by promoting, speaking or offering introductions to speakers you know.

If you don't know where to find a local real estate club meeting, go online and search meetup.com for club meetings in your area; Google "real estate club meeting + your city, or ask any real estate investors you know. Most larger areas have an investment club, but if your area doesn't, why not start one?

CHAPTER ELEVEN

TENANTS, TOILETS, AND TONS OF FUN WITH PROPERTY MANAGERS

Finding and keeping good tenants is actually easier than you might think. It's definitely something you want to do – because tenant turnover is expensive.

Whenever a tenant leaves there is wear and tear to the unit, and it usually means painting, cleaning, and minor repairs *even if you just redid the place.*

Often we try to reduce our costs and not paint or not hire a professional cleaner to make the place shine, but unless we're in a *hot* rental market, we sometimes regret the decision.

TO CLEAN OR NOT TO CLEAN: AN EXAMPLE FROM MARCH 2012

When the tenant gave us notice, we took a look at the property. They had two dogs and a lot of crap strewn about the property, and it did not show well. We knew we'd be wasting our time looking for a good tenant if we showed the property in that state. So we waited until they moved out.

When they moved out, they did clean the place, but a non-professional cleaning job is never as good as a professional one.

In this case, because we hadn't shown it while they lived there, we had a vacant property on our hands and we were anxious to find tenants and start collecting rent. The cash was tight on the property already, so we chose not to take the time or spend the money on a professional cleaning. We went into the house and wiped a few surfaces, had our carpenter fix a few things, brought in a landscaper to deal with the 40 lbs of dog poop that was in the yard, and basically started showing it immediately.

We had half a dozen people go through, and the only tenants that applied were people we didn't want to rent to. We were starting to wonder what the issue was. Then our office manager showed the place for us and got some rather blunt feedback from a prospective tenant. This potentially good candidate bluntly told Allison: "This property isn't well maintained and it's dirty."

With that kind of feedback – which we *never* get on our rentals because we are so particular about the condition we show them in – we had to face the fact that we had been *too* budget conscious and we needed to smarten up.

I didn't agree with that tenant ... the property was well maintained; but her blunt comment forced us to evaluate the property with fresh eyes. Trust me – sometimes you just *do not see* how worn or run down the place looks. Ask your favorite female friend to take a look for you, and ask her if she'd bathe her kids there or look forward to cooking dinner in the kitchen. Her input will tell you a lot!

We should have hired a cleaner, but by the time we reached the conclusion that it needed a really good cleaning we were only five hours away from showing it to four more potential tenants, so we had no time to waste.

Dave and I grabbed all our cleaning supplies and got to work. The price we paid was sore knees, cracked fingers and three hours of scrubbing. After our scrubbing, the property rented right away. Amazing what a thorough cleaning will do.

You would think we wouldn't make mistakes like that at this stage, but the reality is that we don't like to spend money unnecessarily and sometimes we think we can get away without spending it – usually we can't!

Of course there are many other stories. For entertainment and educational purposes, allow us to share with you what can happen if you *don't* follow our suggestions and steps for finding and keeping good tenants. Of course, the best way to minimize tenant problems is to prevent the bad ones from ever moving into your property in the first place! (We learned that the hard way.)

THE TENANT WITH A KNIFE

Our real estate investing life was crashing around us. Dave was in the middle of dealing with fire code violations at two of his properties in Niagara Falls, Ontario, and we'd just moved into our triplex to do a bunch of renovations. We had finished redoing the kitchen in the suite we were living in and we were working on the bathroom. The toilet was actually sitting in the middle of the kitchen floor, out of service, and Dave was shaving over the kitchen sink with a mirror we had propped up on boxes.

Our life was chaotic. The bills for the renovations were more than we'd planned for, and the fines and charges for the violations on the two multiplexes were edging close to $15,000.

Meanwhile, our basement tenant was struggling to find a new roommate, and he was going to have to move out if he wasn't successful. We were not feeling up to the task of renting it out and were worried it would cost us money if we had to go there. Finally he found someone through the "roommates wanted" board at his university.

We checked her credit and there were a few questionable things. She had a great excuse, though – her last landlord had been out to get her – and her story was so elaborate it was be-lievable.

It made sense that we couldn't call her landlord for a refer-ence because things had ended so badly. Before that, she'd sup-posedly been living at home, so we couldn't really get a reference from her parents. She was currently living with a friend while she tried to find her own place.

The red flags were waving in our faces, but our current tenant was a quiet and clean young guy and we wanted him to stay. So we did exactly what you should never do – we ignored the warnings and our gut instinct and let her sign a lease and become a tenant in our basement.

Things were okay for a few weeks. Then the fights started. She had taken over the place with all her stuff; and our neat and tidy tenant was overwhelmed and unhappy. We started to get complaints from each tenant about the other.

We settled the odd dispute between them, but mostly we left things up to them to resolve. We had plenty of real estate and work problems to deal with that didn't involve them.

Then one Thursday night, we heard an incredible commotion beneath us at 2 a.m. We don't know what woke us up first – the doors slamming or the screaming. Our tenants were fighting – and it sounded violent. We could hear crashing noises and swearing, and then our doorbell rang. I pleaded with Dave not to answer the door, but he did. And suddenly he was involved in what became a very long night.

Long story made short: our new tenant had threatened the old tenant with a knife because he had used her telephone. She was reportedly high on drugs, and while the knife turned out to be a butter knife, it was still scary! He called the police and she was taken away. He packed his things and was gone by the time she returned the next morning.

That was when our real problems began. We now had the unstable woman living beneath us. We filed a complaint with the landlord and tenant board regarding the night she was taken away by the police, but because it was only one infraction, she just got a warning. It didn't give us legal grounds to evict her.

When the end of the month came around, she paid her half of the rent. We let her know she was also responsible for the other half of the rent, given that her roommate had moved out.

She argued that since our former tenant shared the lease, he should be responsible for paying us. She had a point, but it was unlikely we'd get money from him. Besides, we wanted her gone.

We filed a notice of non-payment of rent and began the long and costly process of evicting a tenant – a process that is made even more complicated when a tenant knows their specific rights and what they can do to prolong their free stay. She stopped paying rent and did exactly what she needed to do to ensure the job we had ahead of us to get rid of her was as difficult as possible.

She was able to live beneath us rent-free for almost three months before we could legally have her removed from the premises. And, the removal of her and her belongings by way of a Sheriff was going to cost us $250 plus all the fees for the filings we'd had to go through to get to that point.

Our anger was growing each day we had no money coming in from the basement, plus delivering notices to her about the warnings, non-payment of rent and eviction was terrifying. We really had no idea who we were dealing with and we didn't want to find out.

In the end, two days before we could legally get the Sheriff out to remove her from the premises, we got her family to come to Toronto and move her out.

We went to small claims court and were awarded the right to go after her for the rent. We tried sending a collection agency after her to recover the rent but we never saw a penny. The collection agency said her family was evasive and she couldn't be found. Nine years later we've never collected a penny from her.

That's one lesson we definitely learned the hard way. And we never want you to have to go through that kind of experience. So let's go over, in detail, how to rent out your property and avoid this type of situation!

5 STEPS TO RENTING OUT YOUR PROPERTY

Many real estate training programs out there gloss over the importance of finding great tenants. The focus is all on the finding the deals – the exciting parts of real estate that make you money. Unfortunately, without a great tenant or tenants, your life as a real estate investor will be a nightmare – as our tenant with the knife taught us. Since then, we have taken great pains to find good tenants and we have had very few issues – certainly nothing anywhere near as dramatic. So here's a basic process to follow:

Step 1	Step 2	Step 3	Step 4	Step 5
Prepare the unit for showing	Get your paperwork in order	Research the market rents and place your ad	Show your space	Choose your new tenant

The first thing to keep in mind as a landlord is that *this is a business*. You are selling a product – in this case, a place for someone to live. You need to present yourself and your property in a professional light. If you keep that in mind throughout everything you do, you'll find it's easier to attract and keep good tenants.

STEP 1: PREPARE THE UNIT FOR SHOWING

Get your property in show-worthy condition. If the unit is in rough shape, it's always better to take the time to fix it up before you show it to prospective tenants.

Remember – good tenants have choices; and while some may believe you when you say "We're going to be putting in new carpet and painting before you move in," most will just see the disaster zone and look elsewhere.

If you're not sure whether you should do an upgrade, you can do a simple calculation to figure out how many months it will take to pay back your cost. For example, if you are considering adding in-suite laundry, and you can do it for $1,000, and you are sure you can raise the monthly rent by $75/month, then you want to figure out how many months it will take to pay for this addition:

JULIE BROAD • MORE THAN CASHFLOW

> Cost of the repair or improvement: $
>   = # of months it will take for the cost of
>   the repair to be covered.
> Increased rental income from the repair: $

So, in this example, if you add the laundry, your recovery time is 13.33 months:

$$\$1000 / \$75 = 13.33$$

Cost of laundry / higher rental rate with laundry = 13.33 months to pay for.

So, in just over a year, you can cover the cost of the in-suite laundry.

Keep in mind, though, that some things are often necessary whether they pay back quickly or not. If walls have holes in them or the carpet is destroyed, you have to make the unit suitable to live in, or you will attract troublesome tenants that will probably do even more damage.

SUGGESTIONS FOR PREPARATION

- Fill any holes and put a fresh coat of paint on the walls.
- Check all of the doors, locks, electrical outlets, appliances and light bulbs to ensure they are in working order.
- While you are doing this, create a checklist to use when the tenant moves in or out. Include all of the rooms, doors, windows, drapes/blinds/shutters, outlets and light switches, shelving, appliances, etc. When your tenant moves in, you both need to sign off on this sheet – it's required by law in B.C. If you're not sure how to start this sheet, check out www.docstoc.com for examples. Or, check out www.rto.gov.bc.ca and go to the Forms section for examples.
- Replace any exterior door locks. You can either buy and

install new door locks, or take your door knobs (and lock) to your local locksmith to rekey your locks.
- Air the unit out before showing it – open up the doors and windows to let in fresh air.

Since you're doing market research, this is also a good time to note any features your unit might be missing that competitors have. For example, if every other unit in the area has a dishwasher, you should seriously consider putting one in. If all the other rentals in your price range have in-suite washer and dryer units, you might want to look into that. The renters in your area will place different values on different features and amenities, but since you've been doing market research, you will be familiar with what people want or what is most commonly offered. Make sure you are as competitive as possible before you show the unit.

When your current tenant is moving out, and it's been a while since you looked at comparable rentals in the area, take the opportunity to look around to see what other units are renting for and what they are offering. You may be pleasantly surprised to find that rent in comparable units is 10-20% higher than what you had been getting! So you too can ask for a higher rent!

STEP 2: GET YOUR PAPERWORK IN ORDER

To attract good tenants, you will need to be a professional landlord and have the right paperwork on hand. Contact the local residential housing branch of your government or go online and do a search for landlord forms to find the following:

- Tenant application forms
- Rental/lease agreement forms
- Eviction notices or other forms you might need later – sometimes you have to order the forms so it's better to just have them on hand.

- Each provincial and state government has different requirements and rules for what *must* be and what *can* be in each of the above documents, so be careful what you download.

Ensure you've got documents for the province in which your rental unit is located. We also highly recommend you open a new bank account for this property. It may sound like a lot of work at this point, but when you're trying to figure out your income and expenses for the year, and it's mixed in with your personal purchases, it will be a nightmare. And if you spend the damage or security deposit and don't have the money to pay your tenant when they move out, you could face legal action.

STEP 3: RESEARCH THE RENT RATES AND PLACE YOUR AD

In most places in Canada, you will find that using Kijiji and other online sites will be the best way to fill your rentals. If you're targeting seniors, or if you're in a small market where there's a local paper; you'll need to modify my recommendations for what is appropriate for you. But generally speaking, with online ads here's what is absolutely critical:

- Include *great* pictures. I've seen all kinds of hilariously bad photos on MLS and Kijiji for properties for sale and for rent. I've seen ones with people in them, dirty dishes on every inch of counter space, and even pictures of ceilings or doors. If you know nothing about photography, it's time to learn or to hire someone. Good pictures are *critical*. And yes, if you have tenants that redefine the word "pigsty," you should wait until they move out or the unit has been well cleaned.
- Create a compelling title for the ad. Just a little hint here: "3 bdrm, 2 bth, utilities included, near university" is *not* compelling. "A student's dream, 7 minutes to university, spacious & clean" is better. "Tired of gross student

rentals? Steps from university; clean, bright & waiting for you" is even better. Make sure you include inviting details. Then wow them with your pictures and they'll *have* to come and see it.

MAKE SURE THE PRICE IS RIGHT!

Research similar units online to make sure you're not asking too much for your unit. We check Rentometer for a ballpark range, and then research in detail to understand what the competition has their units priced at.

The internet has made detailed research quick and easy. Check out some of these:

- http://hotpads.com U.S. map-based real estate search engine, listing homes for sale, apartments, condos, and rental houses. It also has a buy vs. rent calculator in case you're interested!
- http://www.padmapper.com
- http://www.rentalhomesplus.com Homes for rent all across the U.S.
- http://www.trulia.com U.S. site we use all the time. It has listings, comps and maps all in one place, plus stats and other numbers that we love.
- http://www.kijiji.ca Free online classifieds.
- http://www.rentalproperties.ca Find rental properties all across Canada (Selection is pretty darn limited – but maybe it will get better over time?)
- http://www.rentspot.com Just for Calgary, AB, Canada, but it's a neat tool for finding rental units in Calgary.
- http://viewit.ca Great rental comparisons and they are expanding across Canada (they used to be just in Toronto but their website indicates they are now in many Canadian cities).
- http://www.apartments.com Large database of rentals all across the U.S.

- http://www.rent.com An eBay owned company that you can use to search for rentals, homes and even vacation rentals.
- http://www.craigslist.org Craigslist is everywhere and is cheap or free to post listings, so it typically is the most comprehensive database of rentals.

Don't get too greedy. It's better to price just below the market. *But* if you know you've got a high quality property that will be in demand, don't be afraid to be a little aggressive on your rent rates. We typically get $100 – $150 more per month than a "normal" rental in our area because our properties are the best quality on the market. Test an ad out – if you don't get much response in the first 48 hours and you've created an interesting ad with great pictures, drop the rent quickly by at least $50.

If you're struggling to fill it – drop the rent. Typically, you will rent your unit faster, have a larger tenant base to pick from, and have a better chance of retaining a tenant for a longer period of time if you have lower rent. When you find yourself thinking "but I could easily make $30/month more," counter that thought with "but it will cost me even more if this unit goes vacant for a month, or if I have to re-paint or fix up this unit in 12 months when the current tenant leaves in search of a better deal." Don't leave a stack of money on the table; just know that it's better to be slightly below market and have a great tenant in there quickly than to get a few more dollars every month.

Once you've determined a reasonable market rental rate and your unit is ready for showing, it's time to market that unit!

WHO IS YOUR TARGET RENTER?

Think about who they are, where they work, what they do for fun, and then SELL THEM on why your property is the perfect place for THEM!! Do not try to be all things to all people! Remember – you're an area expert and you already know who is most likely to rent from you, so why not speak directly to them?

GET THE WORD OUT! WE'VE FOUND TENANTS THROUGH ALL OF THE FOLLOWING METHODS:

- **Word of mouth:** We e-mail all our tenants and friends and family that live near the unit that is for rent and let them know about it. As a result, we have rented several units out to friends, and friends of tenants, over the years. If someone refers a good tenant to you, it's a good idea to thank them in some way. Depending on the effort that went into the referral, we may just send a thank you card with a small gift certificate (say $25 for a restaurant or bookstore), or we'll send a nice gift basket that costs somewhere between $50 and $100.
- **Advertise online!** The same places where you looked for comparable units will make great places to advertise.
- **Newspapers:** It's a bit old fashioned to advertise for rent in the newspaper, and if your target market is a student, don't bother. If, however, your target market is young families or older couples without children, then definitely put an ad in your local paper. You'll want to make sure the ad gets attention. Look in the paper and see what ads stand out and try and do something to get the attention of your target audience. The price and the number of bedrooms must be clearly shown, but you may also want to mention location features (e.g., 1 block from bus stop and great restaurants).

> *The medium doesn't make the sale ... the message does. And because 100 percent of the prospects who'll be getting your message are ... well, people – and because human nature never changes – the things you must do to persuade people to buy never change.*
> *~ Clayton Makepeace*

- **Signs on the Lawn:** Besides Kijiji, our second greatest source of tenants is the sign in the window or on the lawn. It lets neighbours and passers-by know that there is a unit for rent. Make sure the phone number is easy to read for someone driving by in a car. You can also consider putting some details on the sign like: "2 bdr, available April 1st" but then you won't be able to reuse the sign. You can buy cheap signs at Staples or Home Depot, but we spent a few more dollars and ordered chloroplast signs that say FOR RENT with our phone number. There are lots of places where you can order chloroplast signs – they look more professional than cardboard written on with black felt pen. We use vistaprint.ca.

- **University or Hospital Housing Boards:** If you're near a large facility like a university or hospital, check around and see if they have a housing board. This is becoming less used as the internet has taken over, but it's still a good spot for the right rentals.

> WHEREVER YOU ADVERTISE, MAKE SURE YOU INCLUDE A PHONE NUMBER– and if you have a website for your rentals, include that too.

STEP 4: SHOWING YOUR SPACE

When you start to receive phone calls or e-mails about your rental property, remember you are selling a product. That product is only partially your rental property. You are also selling yourself as a professional and competent property manager. And you should know the area of this property well.

So be prepared for the calls, and consider making some notes so you're ready to answer the most common questions, which may include:

- What the rent includes or doesn't include (cable, hydro, heat, parking, storage, etc.).
- How close the property is to nearby features and amenities like bus stops, schools, shopping, and recreational facilities.
- When the unit is available.
- How much for a security deposit (or last month's rent) and when it's expected.

- How many parking spaces are available with the unit, and where they are.
- Whether there are laundry facilities nearby or included in the unit (and if they cost anything).
- When they can see the property.

If you have good answers for all of the above, you will sound prepared and competent. Once the tenant has asked any questions they have, it's important to make sure they are a fit for the unit and for your rental program.

Here are the questions we ask before we set up a time for them to view the property:

1) Are you renting now?
2) Why are you considering moving?
3) Are you happy with your current landlord? Why or why not?
4) Who will be living in the property?
5) Do you have any pets, and if so, what types?
6) Do you work in the area?

If there is anything about your suite that could turn them off, mention it upfront to save yourself the effort of showing them. For example, we have a suite that only has a shower – no bathtub. After showing it to one person who said he needed a bathtub, we realized we needed to mention the lack of a tub when a potential tenant called. As it turned out, about half of the potential tenants wanted a bathtub, so we saved ourselves a lot of hassle coordinating showings by letting people know that detail up front.

We generally try to schedule all our showings for the same time. When a tenant calls about seeing the unit, tell them that you will have a showing for all interested tenants at time slot one; and then if it's still available, there will be a second showing. If someone can't make it to the first one, get their **name and phone number so you can call them if there is a second showing!**

You *could* show your unit to one tenant at a time. This is a great way to get to know the applicant a bit more, but it is also very time-consuming and inefficient, especially if you don't live nearby. Also, an open house-like environment creates an air of demand, which helps get applications completed much quicker. When a prospective tenant sees the other interested parties ... if they want your unit, they will act quickly and try to get it. Encourage the prospective tenants to complete the rental application before they leave. Then you will have the application in hand and you can make notes on the application about who they were and what your initial impressions of them were. Alternatively, ask them to drop off, fax or email the application the next day (especially if you've already received other applications).

We have some highly rated videos on YouTube that take you step-by-step through showing your property. Here's one Dave filmed on a way to review your tenant applications and pick the best candidates: http://youtu.be/eW17J9NW9pg

View it (and over 100 others) at: **http://youtube.com/revnyou**.

STEP 5: I CHOO...CHOO...CHOOSE YOU! CHOOSE YOUR
NEW TENANT

When your open house is over, and you have a handful of applications, make notes about which candidates you liked the best. If you don't think there were enough people there, or if you weren't happy with the applications that came in, run your second showing.

Once you have a handful of applications:

1. *Review the applications of the candidates that gave you the best impression.* Look for gaps where a place of residence is not indicated and look for conflicting information. If you liked them, but there are gaps or issues with their application, ask them about it. If you start to hear things like

"well, my previous landlord didn't like me because of..." or "there is a credit agency after me because of..." it's not a great start. Some reasons make complete sense; others are just elaborate stories. If you can't be sure which is which, keep looking – or, like us, you could end up with a tenant that pulls a knife on another tenant!

2. *Run a credit check: (Make sure your rental applications ask for permission to run credit checks on your prospective tenants!)* Once you've found one or two prospective tenants that you like and that have a good application, run a credit check. This is a critical piece. Many veteran landlords say they just trust their gut. Well, we trust our gut, and then verify it! Most provinces and states have services where you can do credit checks. We run ours through an association we belong to called ROMS BC. They also provide some interpretation of what the credit check means.

3. *There is also a company called TVS (Tenant Verification Services) that runs credit checks (www.tenantverification.com).* There's always a fee for credit checks, and we typically pay somewhere between $7 and $15 per applicant. If you go through a one-time service like TVS you'll pay twice that. If you have two people moving in make sure you check the credit of both. It will be twice the price, but knowing the credit and history of both tenants is crucial.

CREDIT CHECK: THINGS TO WATCH FOR

- Does their story line up with their credit history? Before you run their credit, ask them a simple question like "Is there anything I should know about your credit report?" or "Will anything come up on your credit report that I should know about?" If they say no and it turns out to be a mess, that is a GIANT red flag. If they say yes and disclose the situation, then at least they are honest.
- Have they used most of their credit room? For example, if they have a $10,000 Visa Limit and a $20,000 Line of Credit, and both are maxed out, we wouldn't rent to them. If they have less than half used up, we would be comfortable.
- Have they been pretty consistent about making payments?

We were filling a property that was in *high* demand. Our first choice was a couple with two young boys. They were well dressed, they drove a nice truck, and he had a good job and was being relocated to our city with the same company. We figured they were the best candidates. When we ran their credit, however, we discovered a complete mess! They had seven different credit collection notices, including one for an adult movie store for a few hundred dollars! Needless to say, we decided to pass on renting to them – but we suggested they take a look at their credit report because there were a lot of issues in there.

4. *Reference checks*: Call the reference and ask them simple questions like: "How long have you known the applicant?" "What's your relationship with them?" and "Would you rent to them?" This is also a good gut check, but keep in mind that a current landlord might be anxious to get rid of a not-so-great tenant and therefore might not tell you the entire truth. If the tenants did not live together previously, call references for both tenants.

We generally don't call current landlords for reference checks – we call the one *before* the current one. We also don't tend to call the employer's number given to us on the application; instead, we find the number online or in the phone book and call that number. You never know what has been made up, and you need to just take little steps like that to ensure you're not simply calling a friend who says the would-be tenant is great!

When you have selected a candidate, call them immediately and ask them to sign the lease and provide their security deposit. Don't allow them more than 48 hours to get this to you, and don't call the other interested candidates to tell them it's rented until this is done. You have to move quickly once you have applications in hand. Everyone wants to know if they have a place to live and you want to be assured of getting it filled. *If you're too slow, the other applicants will find other places.*

THREE TIPS FOR HANDLING TOUCHY TENANTS

You will never get into trouble by admitting that you may be wrong. That will stop all argument and inspire your opponent to be just as fair and open and broadminded as you are. It will make him want to admit that he, too, may be wrong.
~ *Dale Carnegie,* How to Win Friends and Influence People

I love it when a tenant is happy, and my husband and I work hard to give our tenants a great home to live in at a fair rent rate. But I've also stopped trying to please every single tenant because financially that doesn't make sense, and because some tenants just aren't going to be happy no matter what you do.

Take the example I had recently of a tenant who asked to have road access to her garage. The home had a garage in the back alley but the yard was fenced. Previous occupants had used it as a workshop and didn't need access via the alley, but our tenant wanted to store a boat in there so she needed to be able to drive into it.

We figured we could turn the fence into a gate, no problem, but when our carpenter went to do that, it wasn't as simple as we thought. It would be a huge pain to swing the gate open and closed. Instead, I decided to simply move the fence to open up the garage. Our tenant's yard was still fully fenced but it was a little smaller because we now had the garage door open to the alley.

Our tenant was absolutely furious. She screamed at me on the phone:

"I hate it! I absolutely hate it. Now when my garage door is open I have to make sure my child doesn't wander into the alley and get hit by a car. It's just not safe now. I feel so exposed. I don't know why you didn't consult with me about it. I have no privacy now. It's totally ruined my back yard."

It took a while to calm her down, but by the end of the conversation she was thanking me for getting her access to the garage so quickly and she apologized for freaking out.

So what did that look like for me?

Believe me, it wasn't easy. Every bone in my body was getting defensive, my temperature was rising, and I went from feeling calm to feeling agitated. But I bit my tongue and let her speak. And I followed these principles:

1. No matter how hard it is – do not get involved in an argument. Even when you know the other person is wrong, avoid saying so. Instead, ask yourself, "What is to be gained by proving them wrong?" Usually the answer is your own sense of pride – which really isn't that important. What is always more important is the relationship.
2. When you are wrong – even in the slightest way – admit it wholeheartedly and quickly.

> *Any fool can try to defend his or her mistakes – and most fools do – but it raises one above the herd and gives one a feeling of nobility and exultation to admit one's mistakes.*
>
> *~ Dale Carnegie*

3. Let the other person talk more than you do, and listen. Really listen and try to see how you would feel in their shoes. Consider their viewpoint, be sympathetic even, and you'll usually have a much easier time staying calm and listening to the other person, and the other person will feel truly heard – which 9 times out of 10 solves the problem anyway.

I didn't offer to fix the fence or do anything further; I simply listened. And when I was done listening, I acknowledged my responsibility in the situation, apologized for what I had done, and let her know that I could see where she was coming from.

I saved a ton of energy and time by not arguing, and I didn't have to spend any money fixing something that didn't have to be fixed. I made the problem go away with some simple alterations to how I handled the initial conversation. Maybe these tips will help you next time you're dealing with a touchy tenant.

CHAPTER TWELVE

MANAGING YOUR PROPERTY OR YOUR PROPERTY MANAGER

I think it's a great idea to manage your first investment property for a while, so you can get a solid understanding of what's involved. You'll know what makes a great property manager and have a better appreciation for how challenging the job can be. That said; managing your own properties may not be the right thing for you.

To find out if you could handle the pressures and challenges of property management, you'll want to do a bit of a self-assessment. Think about your answers to the following questions:

- Are you a reasonably tolerant person? Be honest with yourself.

- Do you have any knowledge and experience with doing minor maintenance and repairs?
- Are you able to sell and negotiate? You'll have to sell the unit to renters; you'll have to sell the idea of paying rent on time; and you'll have to have the problem solving and negotiation skills of a salesperson in order to handle some of the issues that will arise.
- Can you visit the property on a regular basis? You should stop by monthly (at least for the first few months of a new tenancy), so make sure it's possible and convenient to do so. Plus, if you do get a 3 a.m. call that requires you to get there right away, are you going to be able to?
- Are you capable of keeping good records? This is not usually an enjoyable part of the job, but it is absolutely necessary!
- Are you able to deal with angry individuals and ease the tension between them? How do you handle difficult or angry people? When dealing with a difficult or angry person, do you get angry and frustrated yourself?
- Imagine the busiest possible day, and then imagine having to handle a call from one of your tenants about a frozen pipe or a broken door lock. Are you going to be able to handle that situation?
- Do you have someone that can be your back-up if you take a vacation or go out of town? If there's an emergency at your property, your tenants need to be able to get in touch with someone that can make decisions about the property.

If you answer "no" or "I don't know" to three or more of these questions, you should seriously consider hiring someone to help with your property management.

HIRING PROFESSIONAL PROPERTY MANAGERS

Consider hiring professional property management for your properties when you have any of the following:

- Multiple properties in a market area – unless you're ready to hire help in your real estate business or you're not working at a full time job;
- A building with more than six units;
- And/or when you live far away (several hours) from your property.

The only exception is if you can find a trusted friend to live at the property and help you manage it.

If you're ready to hire a professional, here's how we recommend you do it:

STEP 1: GET REFERRALS

This can be tricky if you don't know any other real estate investors in the area where you've purchased your property, but here are a few tips for getting referrals:

- Go to a local real estate investing club (local to your property, that is) and ask them.
- Ask friends and family if they know anybody that has property in the area of your investment. Then, ask if you can speak to that person.
- Ask your real estate agent, mortgage broker, and/or lawyer if they can recommend any property managers.

You can also check with local organizations. In BC, we are members of ROMS BC http://www.suites-bc.com/. Do a search for property management organizations or for renter and owner associations for your city. Generally these types of organizations will not be able to recommend a company to you but you can see who is a member and start contacting them that way at least.

You are looking for the smaller to midsize firms that will take on a single family house; not large property management companies that just manage big apartment or commercial buildings.

Be tenacious!

Today, the internet is incredibly powerful. Blogs, forums and customer feedback websites are everywhere, and it's pretty easy to uncover happy or unhappy reports about just about anyone or anything. So, hit the internet and search for property managers in your market area, or get the local phone book and find property management companies. Check the Better Business Bureau for any bad reports. **Utilize resources like Twitter and Facebook as well.** Send out a message asking others if they know of the company that you're considering hiring. Solicit private feedback about their experience working with particular companies.

By doing a simple web search, you will likely uncover the property manager's website and also other websites referring to them, and you may learn a little bit about them (good or bad). When you combine that with a little research via social media, you should quickly be able to collect information that will help you make a wise decision.

STEP 3: CALL THEM

What you want to find out at this point is:

1. **What types of properties do they manage?** Do they manage single family properties, duplexes, triplexes, other types? Do they specialize in the area or property type that you specialize in?
2. **Do they offer services other than property management?** Ask the question exactly this way – you want to make it sound like you are looking for an all-purpose firm, *but you're not!* If the best property manager you find is inside a real estate agency, that's okay. What you're trying to avoid is:
   - A real estate agent that says he/she will help you out with property management *just so you will buy or sell*

property with them. They won't have the same credentials or expertise that a professional property manager has.

- A company that has their own contracting business. You want them to have access to good service professionals like electricians, handymen and plumbers; but if part of their business is repairing properties, how can you be certain that all repairs they do are necessary or that they are charged out at market rates? If they *do* have their own contracting company, you may want to ask them if they always get two or more estimates before proceeding with the work.

3. **What do they charge?** What other fees do they have on top of their management fee? For example, some management companies will charge you 10% of your rental income each month to manage the property; but in addition to this fee you will also pay for anything extra like advertising for new tenants, tenant credit checks, and sometimes even a document processing fee in order to get monthly statements. Other property management companies will charge 10% *plus* half a month's rent to place a tenant, but that will include any fees involved with the tenant attraction and selection process. *Every company prices themselves differently* and you need to find out what each company will cost you if you don't already know. If their fees seem really cheap, find out why. Will they make a profit from you in another way?

4. **Ask them for references in the area.** Say you'd like references that you can call, and in each case ask for the address of the property they manage as well as the person's name and number. See "Step 4: A little more research" (below) regarding this item.

5. **Confirm that the company carries the necessary insurance.** They are going to be handling your rent money, so they need to be appropriately bonded and insured.

Take a walk by a few of the properties they manage. You may find a few tenants hanging around that you can chat with. Even if you don't find anybody around to speak to, you can still get a good sense of how the property is being maintained.

Next, you want to call the references you were given. Here's what you should ask them:

- Are you happy with the services of the property manager?
- Would you hire them for another property if you purchased another one?
- Is there anything I should be aware of in working with them?
- How long have they been managing your property?
- How did you learn about their services?

STEP 5: MAKE AN AGREEMENT

I recently had a coaching call with someone who was asking me all kinds of questions regarding what he could do about some property management issues he had – but he had signed a contract that he had *never* read. He actually didn't understand what services he was being charged for!

Most management companies will have a standard agreement for you to sign. If you're just starting out, you probably don't want to have to pay to create your own, and one from online may not be very good. So it's not necessarily a bad thing to use the standard agreement the management company provides, *but make sure you read each and every word in that document before you sign it!* If there is something you don't understand, ask a lawyer!

Ensure you understand all of the services they are promising to provide, and make sure they have detailed:

- The reports you will receive and when you can expect to receive them.
- Management fees, including charges for renting vacant units, advertising, cleaning, or any other additional fees (like snow removal or yard maintenance, if applicable).
- The services they will provide to your tenants (24/7 tenant response is a must!).

A few things that you may want to think about:

- No fee charged for vacant units: This can work both ways. If your property manager only gets paid when the unit is filled, there is a greater incentive to ensure your property is always occupied. However, you may find your property manager rushes to fill units, accepting unqualified candidates that cost you more in the long run.
- Long-term contracts: Some property managers may wish to have a multi-year agreement with you, and in exchange you will get better rates. However, you may want to give the company a test run before you agree to this. A property manager that knows they have to consistently deliver good service or lose your business is more motivated than one that has your business tied up for several years.
- Signing their standard agreement without having a lawyer review it: A property manager's agreement is going to be written to their benefit. If you read it and are unsure of anything, get legal advice.

HOW TO PREVENT YOUR PROPERTY MANAGERS FROM ROBBING RENT MONEY FROM YOU

Dave noticed the water bill on one of our rental properties was double what it usually is. He immediately contacted our property manager and asked that it be checked out.

Turns out we had a water leak. The leak was quickly fixed and the next water bill was back around its normal amount. We paid the water bill on that little split level with a one-bedroom basement suite, so Dave's swift action saved us hundreds of dollars.

We weren't always on top of our properties like this. We've learned the hard way that it's just as important to manage your property manager as it is to carefully run your numbers before you buy a property.

So, what can you do to ensure you catch the little "leaks" that can cost you hundreds over time and make sure you're not missing out on rent money because of missteps by your property manager or managers?

KNOW BEFORE YOU BUY

Even if you plan to manage the property yourself, chat with local property managers before you buy a property. They can confirm the rent rates, identify potential issues with an area or a property, and – most importantly – they can let you know if they would manage the property if you need a manager in the future. Not every property manager will manage every type of property.

Our entire Niagara Falls experience was largely because we bought properties in areas that none of the professional property management companies in town would manage. Of course we didn't realize that until *after* we already owned them. We ended up contacting the seller of the properties and asking him for a referral. We hired the only guy that would do the job. After he was charged with manslaughter and we had to handle the fire code violations, we were forced to let him go and find someone else. Again, we had to hire the only guy that would manage our properties. His inexperience cost us a lot of time and money lost on vacancies. He used a $5,000 renovation budget to partially renovate *two* units instead of fully renovating *one* unit. We then had two units that we couldn't rent out because they were unfinished, instead of one complete unit and one incomplete unit.

Now we *always* interview multiple property managers before we buy in a new area.

If you've ensured that there are competent and reputable property managers willing to manage the property you're about to buy, then you know you have a back-up plan if you can't continue on as manager.

GET COPIES OF EVERYTHING!

After owning a triplex in the Little Italy area of Toronto for several years, we decided to move in and renovate the kitchen and bathroom in two of the three units. We let our property manager go and proceeded to collect the rent from the third unit ourselves. When the tenants delivered the cheque to our door, it was $100 more than we were expecting.

We didn't have copies of the signed leases. The only thing we could prove was that the property manager's statements we had been receiving indicated we were taking in rent that was $100 less than what the tenants were paying us. We now suspect he'd been pocketing up to $200 of extra rent money each month as well as billing us for maintenance that wasn't done.

Now we obtain, and keep copies of, every single lease. We ask for copies of the rent cheques and rent receipts, and we ask for before-and-after photos of any maintenance work that is done. We no longer take the property manager's monthly statement as proof of what revenue our property is generating.

NEVER IGNORE A VACANCY

The fewer tenant turnovers you deal with on a property, the more money you'll make. But just as important as monitoring your turnover is keeping a close eye on any vacant units you have.

As soon as you find out a unit is going to be sitting vacant, start asking questions and schedule a walk-through. It's a good idea to check out the inside of your property periodically anyway, but if it's not renting out quickly then you want to find the issue that is preventing the unit from renting. It could be the marketing; it could be the asking rent rate, a shift in the overall rental market, or the way the unit looks.

A few years back, a property we'd owned for nearly eight years was sitting vacant. We'd never had an issue renting this unit out in the past. The property manager explained that the rental market was slow because many of the new houses and condos were being rented out by the builders until the market picked up and they could sell them.

This property manager had always been excellent and his explanation made sense, so we let the first month of vacancy go. But when we learned that the unit was going to be vacant for a second month, we arranged a walk-through and started asking questions. It turned out that the property looked tired and needed new kitchen countertops, flooring and paint. The yard was also a mess and needed some major landscaping work.

Immediately after the walk-through, we got organized to do a small renovation. A week later, and only a few days into the renovation project, we already had new tenants for the property.

Even if you've been working with an excellent property manager for nearly eight years, check out each and every vacancy. Remember that nobody cares about your money more than you do!

KNOW THY NEIGHBOURS

We lived in Vancouver and owned properties in Toronto. That can be a bit tricky when you want to check up on what's going on with your properties.

One of the ways we like to keep an eye on what is going on with our properties is to get to know our neighbours. If we can, we introduce ourselves as the owners of the property next door, and we let them know that if there is something going on at the property that they don't like, we probably wouldn't like it either. We also make a point to stop by and bring them little gifts when we're in town to thank them for watching over our place.

DO A MONTHLY BILL AND STATEMENT REVIEW

My husband Dave spends several hours every month reviewing every utility, tax, maintenance and property management bill we receive on each and every property. Because he does this monthly, it's easy for him to spot things that are out of the ordinary. He contacts our property managers promptly with questions or concerns; and if there are problems, we create a plan of action to handle the issue swiftly and cost effectively.

We work with *great* property managers now. Most of the time there are very few things we need to get involved with. But we've learned that no matter how good the property manager is, *nobody else* loves and cares for our properties and money like we do. And now that we're actively managing our property managers, we're making a whole lot more money than we did before.

> *Remember, you can earn more money, but when time is spent it's gone forever.*
>
> ~ *Zig Ziglar*

CHAPTER THIRTEEN

SYSTEMS FOR SUCCESS

W hen someone is getting you all excited about doing deals, they don't tell you that the more properties you own the more complicated your life will become. Every property is another heating, electrical or plumbing system that can have problems. Each and every roof you own is a whole pile of receipts, leases, documents and notations to be filed, organized and submitted to the tax man. Nobody tells you that when you're starting out, because it doesn't get you excited about investing in real estate and it shouldn't. If you don't have it under control – even if you just have a few properties, let alone dozens – it sucks.

Surrounded by piles of paper –some labeled but most not – and exhausted from hours and hours of data entry, I couldn't help but cry.

We hadn't stayed on top of the data entry for our dozen or so properties. In previous years, I would sit down once a month and enter in rents and expenses for the properties I was in charge of, and my husband Dave would do the same for the ones he was responsible for. But that year (2006) we'd let everything slide.

We'd moved from Toronto to Vancouver, which was a big event; plus I had a very busy job that saw me traveling for at least a week every month – sometimes longer; plus (and this was really the biggest reason) neither of us liked doing it.

Once we missed a few months, the task seemed so much more daunting the next month; so we ignored it again.

Before we knew it, over 12 months had passed and it was tax time. So we couldn't put it off any longer. It was just paper – we knew it wouldn't kill us – but it was awful and sometimes we felt like we were being buried alive.

After that debacle, we agreed we would revise our business processes so we were never faced with that dilemma again. We also agreed that there were other areas of our business that needed attention. *Chaos was costing us money, wasting our time and making us miserable.*

One of the big changes we made was who we used for accounting; we'd been using a small business accountant that Dave's family used, but when we added rent to own to our portfolio, it became clear we needed a real estate investing specialist. We also hired a bookkeeper; and then once I was doing real estate full time, we reviewed every area where we could make more money and reduce our expenses.

We focused on:

- Creating a simple but effective filing system to minimize the number of times any one document was handled and reduce the time it took to find any document we needed to reference;
- Bringing property management duties in-house (see more about this below) so the money saved could be put towards hiring someone to work in our office and handle all the tasks neither of us wanted to do;
- Creating a checklist and database of team members, their roles, where we learned about them, and our relationship with them;
- Streamlining marketing so that we were finding deals and tenants easily and without interrupting our spare time.

Today there are still parts of the business that I have to be involved in but that I don't love (e.g., babysitting contractors on renovation projects, handling tenant troubles like a legal grow-op that we uncovered), and I know Dave would say the same (he's the one that deals with insurance and the banks!). But for the most part, our business is now set up so that we can buy and sell and manage our properties with less stress compared to our first couple of years (and, most of the time, more profit too!).

But just because we have systems in place to reduce our stress doesn't mean there isn't any. And truthfully, buying 10-12 houses a year got tiring after only a few years of going at that pace. In 2012, we slowed down and only bought six houses. In 2013, as I write this, I wouldn't be surprised if we acquire fewer than six houses. It's a ton of work, even with a great system and in-office help; and as I have already mentioned, we're not passionate about real estate. We both have passions outside of real estate that we want to focus on (like writing books to help you!).

Regardless, systems are important whether you own two rentals or twenty-two. It allows you to profit from your properties and live your life comfortably with less worry.

Some investors get far more sophisticated than we do with their systems and processes. They buy software, create elaborate check lists, and hire virtual assistants. You can do that too, and for many it's the right thing – but we tend to lean toward the simpler and often easier to control options. It depends on your personality and what you want to spend time and money on … but for us this is working and some of these ideas just might help you too – whether you're going full time or not.

1. SIMPLE BUT EFFECTIVE FILING SYSTEM

We used to use one binder per property, but we found that as we owned a place for several years, the binder started to burst. Files are simpler and easier to manage. We now have an "inbox" where all mail and documents sit until they've been processed (scanned so our bookkeeper can enter them in). Then we have four file folders for each property:

- Legal documents (purchase agreement, mortgage docs)
- Tenants (their application, lease, and any communications)
- Important docs like warranties and insurance
- Income, expenses & receipts (bank statements, repairs).

At the end of each year, the expense file is labeled with the year and property address and put away into our "if we are ever audited" tax box for that year. Every tenant turnover results in the creation of a new file and the filing away of that tenant file. Every document is scanned and stored *online* as well.

Storing the documents online and creating a "virtual office" has been a huge help to us. No matter where in the world we are, as long as we have our iPad and internet connection, we can handle anything. There are now so many options for storing your files online – from Dropbox to clouds to back-up services – it just depends on the security features and access needs that you have.

2. BRINGING PROPERTY MANAGEMENT IN-HOUSE

The decision to bring most of our property management in-house came as the solution to two major problems....

As we started buying properties more aggressively (going from 2-5 per year to 10-12 per year), we found ourselves drowning in paper. From listing sheets of properties we viewed (we have months where we look at more than 50 different properties) right through to lease agreements, insurance documents, mortgage and bank statements, and agreements of purchase and sale – we had dozens of documents for every deal we did, and half as many from the ones we ended up not doing.

We had a good filing system by then, but it required us to actually spend time filing. We found ourselves stacking, piling and tucking stuff in files or drawers to file later. It was bad; when you needed to find something, it was sheer luck if you found it in less than 15 minutes.

That was Part One of the issue. Part Two was that the more time we spent evaluating the performance of our properties and our property managers – the more areas we identified for improvement. From ads placed in the wrong places or not at all, to pictures that would scare away good tenants, to missed maintenance work – we found all kinds of opportunities to do a better job managing our properties ourselves.

The problem was we didn't want to take all the tenant calls.

We decided to take back control of most of our properties and then hire someone into our business to help us.

The math worked. We were paying most of our property managers 10% of monthly rent plus half a month's or a full month's rent to fill vacancies. If we no longer used a property manager, that money could be used to pay a staff member – someone that could help us with property management *and* handle the filing problem.

It was a bigger process than I have space to explain here, but the basics were:

- We identified properties that we could put into our rent-to-own program. As the target properties became vacant, we took them over from our PM and turned them into rent to own.
- We sold a few properties that were far away and causing us stress or were no longer providing us great returns.
- We hired someone who would come into our office to handle all our files, take calls, answer emails, and start to learn all the office work required to self-manage our properties.
- As we added new properties, we handled the property management ourselves, using our new office assistant to take on as much of the work as possible but leaving us to handle the tenant showings and screening.
- We focused on creating simple systems to streamline the process when a tenant moved in, moved out, or had a maintenance issue; or when we had to handle an issue like a noise complaint or non-payment of rent. We created checklists and spreadsheets to keep track of all the critical pieces.

This has been the single most important change to our business; and while it's not always ideal to be self-managing so many of our own properties, we have found that – with help and simple systems – we are able to go away and not worry about what is happening with our tenants in our absence. We also do not have any stress at tax time because everything is organized, entered into Quickbooks, and ready to ship to the accountant. And if something *is* missing, it's not us that have to track down the document!

3. THERE IS NO "I" IN "TEAM"

To be able to do a large volume of deals requires a strong team. Even having a smaller portfolio of properties requires a strong team. Key members of our team today are:

- Great trades people
- Realtor
- Property manager (while we self-manage many of our properties, we do need some help with a few of them!)
- Accountant
- A lawyer and a notary
- Our office manager / assistant
- Broker and/or banker
- Home inspector
- Insurance broker.

I already mentioned this, but I chuckle at the training programs out there that basically say things like: "first, you build your team." Eleven years into it, we're still building our team.

Your team is not a static thing. But it is a critical thing. Without the right advice or the right person, you'll overpay for work, make mistakes, and possibly get into bigger issues like legal challenges. I'd much rather spend $500 on the right advice than try to do it cheap or for free and take unnecessary risks.

Here are three things to keep in mind when you are looking for a new team member:

- Find someone that is recommended – ideally by more than one person.
- Create a database (we just use an Excel spreadsheet) that notes how you found out about them, what properties you worked with them on, what they charge, and what type of payment they will accept (some are okay with credit cards but many want cheques – you'll often want to know this).
- Work on getting back-ups for trades, insurance, and brokers/banks. Sometimes your favourite is busy or the job is bigger and you need quotes. You need to have options

so you don't scramble in the heat of the moment and work with someone that isn't one of your top choices.

4. MARKETING SYSTEMS

How many times do you start from scratch when you have to write an ad? Or worse, how many times do you just go onto Kijiji and copy some other poorly created ad to place an ad for a tenant or find a deal?

We used to be poorly organized with our photos and ads, so we'd have to recreate them every time. That slows things down and often something that worked well in the past will work well again, so it's better to just use it again and again until it doesn't work.

On your computer, have a marketing file *for each property*, where you store *good* photos (clean, free of tenants' junk, and with good lighting), ads that worked, and any of the property details you'll need when you advertise it (size, features, heating type, rough utility cost if applicable). Keep a scanned copy of the MLS listing if you bought a listed property; the details on the listing sheet will come in handy for years to come!

The other three important marketing systems we put into place:

- So we don't get disturbed at all hours. If you use your cell phone for ads, expect to have your personal life and personal time disappear very quickly. Companies like Evoice and Network Telsys have good, inexpensive systems.
- This is especially important if you're paying for any advertising. Track the results all the way through to determine who you end up renting to. For example, by doing this, we found that while we received a lot of calls from Craigslist, all our renters actually came

from Kijiji, and none of them came from the local paper. Now we know where to put our time and money when we're advertising.

- An educational website for our rent to own business – to minimize the time we spend training our prospective tenants on how our program works. We funnel all leads through that website, and it significantly increases the quality of candidates that contact us and reduces the time we spend educating them. Now when a candidate walks through the door, we can get right down to whether they are a good fit for us and whether they qualify.

From the beginning, we could have made things so much easier on ourselves by implementing simple systems, but the reality is that it's so easy to *not* make it a priority.

I've also seen investors go the other way and be *system crazy* when they don't need to be.

For most real estate investors, I believe that a balance between outsourcing as many of the tasks you despise and ensuring you can still control the process and the costs, will be the best solution. And really, the best way to figure out what you will and won't put up with, is to start simple and add more systems as you grow. It now makes sense for us to have an employee in our office because we have a sizeable portfolio and are adding around 10 new homes a year. That wouldn't make sense for most investors, but many could use a part-time bookkeeper, a great filing system, and some spreadsheets to track their team members.

Whatever you choose to implement, make sure it's *helping* you – and may you *never* have to feel like you're being buried alive by paper.

SUPER IMPORTANT TIP #1: Before you put a receipt in your wallet, *write on it*. Include the address of the property and what the receipt was for. For example, if it's a sink for 123 Profit Street, note that before you put it in your wallet. If you just had lunch with your JV Partner on 456 Cashflow Road, write the full names of the folks present, what you discussed, and what property it pertains to. Unless you only own one property, it's *really* hard to remember what was what at the end of the month. Also, if you shop somewhere and buy stuff for your own home and your rental at the same time; put it on two separate bills and label the one that is relevant to your rental. It will make your record keeping so much easier.

SUPER IMPORTANT TIP #2: Open a separate bank account for *every* property you buy. This ensures that all the expenses and rent that applies to one property is easily tracked inside that one account. It might sound like too much effort/cost if you only own a couple of properties – but when you own a lot, it can be hard to know who paid their rent and who didn't. It can also be difficult to figure out *what properties are actually making money* if they are all mixed together. With one bank account per property, all of that is simplified and very obvious. It will also speed up your bookkeeping. Most importantly – *do not use a personal account* for your revenue properties. Trying to remember what withdrawals were personal and what ones were an expense is a very unnecessary nightmare.

There are lots of low/no-fee bank accounts now, so you can minimize your bank fees. And most banks will waive monthly fees if you keep a balance over a certain threshold for the month (usually $2,000 or more – check with your banker).

CHAPTER FOURTEEN

WHERE ARE THE LADIES?

I've had the honour of being a keynote speaker or a panelist at some significant real estate and investment events across Canada. In many cases I've been the only female speaker. Sometimes the female speakers make up about 10-15% of the speaker roster in a larger event – but never more than 25%. The audience is usually 40% female, so it's not that there aren't women investors.... So ladies, why aren't we stepping up more often in a business where, I believe, we are exceptionally gifted? I think it's time to show the world that real estate is a business we're made for!

From the curb, we could see that the yard of this average-looking two-storey home was overgrown, but the sun was shining all around, making it look warm and inviting. Yet, when my husband Dave and I pulled into the driveway, it was as if my blood went cold.

"I don't like this house," I told Dave with a shiver.

He laughed as he was getting out of the car and said, "It just needs a grass cutting and a little landscaping."

Then his mom, Karen, who had been following us in her car, got out of the car, walked up to the front steps, froze in place, and said "There is something really wrong with this house."

Karen and I walked in the front door and up the stairs inside, and then we did a 180-degree turn and walked right back out the front door.

On our checklist, the house had everything:

- It was in our #1 area where we own 60% of our investment properties. In fact, we own the property next door!
- It was built by the same builder who had built half the houses we own. We love the layouts, know his construction, and know where to watch for weaknesses.
- The house had a 70's décor, which meant it hadn't been touched since it was built, which was perfect.

It wasn't the condition of the home that had us running out of that place – the house gave us the creeps.

Dave and our male realtor were laughing at us and commenting about how "women sure are a funny bunch, aren't they?" Neither one of them felt anything.

I didn't need to see any more of the house to know I was never going to buy it, and neither did Karen.

It's been two years since we looked at that house, and since then it has sold once, been rented out, and now it's back on the market again. Work has been done to it, but the weird feeling is still there. And given the price dropping on MLS yet again, it's clearly not just Karen and I feeling it.

Call it women's intuition, or call it craziness – all I know is that I get a "feeling" from houses. Usually it's neutral, sometimes it's really good, sometimes it just doesn't feel quite right, and every once in awhile it's spine-tingling and shiver-inducing bad.

I know a lot of females that have had similar experiences when looking at properties.

All Dave knows is that if I get a bad feeling about a house, other females (tenants and future buyers) are going to be turned off too.

The only deals we've ever lost money on were deals where

Dave and I didn't buy in agreement. Together we pick solid investment opportunities that attract awesome tenants, make money and keep our troubles to a minimum.

Generally, the same goes for tenants, partners or anybody else we're dealing with. Unless we have previous history with someone, Dave relies on me to meet people and get a gut feeling about them. I don't even have to speak with someone for more than a few minutes to be able to check in to my gut reaction.

Scientific? Not at all. Accurate? Almost every single time.

I'm not saying guys can't do this, but I am saying that I know this to be more common to females than males. And I know Dave looks to me for input on people and houses every time because he doesn't read them like I do.

I don't think it's better or worse to be a female or a male; but it's different. That's why I think some of the strongest real estate teams take advantage of the natural skills and tendencies we have as opposite sexes to make for a wickedly powerful duo. (Then again, I am probably biased because Dave and I invest together and have for over a decade!)

But – if you're a woman and you're thinking of getting into this business on your own ... know that you're not actually alone! And know that you have some cool strengths you can draw on to become hugely successful as an investor. Also, real estate investing provides a tremendous opportunity to create financial stability while having flexibility to be at home for your kids and family when you're needed.

Besides the obvious financial benefit of being a real estate investor, many women investors I work with say that their favourite part of being in real estate is the opportunity to tap into their creative side and make money from it. Making something lovely out of something ugly can be very rewarding. Others have said that it makes them feel really good to offer good quality and clean housing to families in their community. And just about every single one mentions that there is a tremendous opportunity to stand out and be noticed as a female in this business. That may not seem advantageous at first; but if you stand out, people will bring potential deals to you, be attracted to you as an investment partner, and be willing to work for you or with you.

And when you roll up to the curb of a house that gives you the creeps, or you get a bad feeling about a tenant – *listen to your gut* – move on and say *"thank you "* for that intuition or craziness that keeps us ladies safe and out of trouble.

TIPS FOR WOULD-BE WOMEN INVESTORS

1. Build your team: Find great people who will complement your skills.
2. Create a support network at home: Most women are caregivers to several people. You'll need support at home to ensure all your loved ones are taken care of when you need to focus on your business. Support can be in the form of a husband, partner, family member, or just discussions with your children so they give you an hour of uninterrupted thinking time.
3. Listen to your gut: Many people – not just women – have a gut instinct that will steer them clear of bad deals if they listen. Women, in particular, often ignore this because they think they're bringing emotion into a deal. The reality is that even a deal with great numbers can be a bad one, and if you listen to your gut you will probably avoid those bad deals disguised by good numbers.
4. Don't over-think it: No deal will be perfect. Find one that is good and get it done. You'll learn from it and become a better and better investor with every deal you do.
5. Have fun with it: Don't take it too seriously if someone asks if they can speak to your husband. Smile and say, "You can, but he won't know what you're talking about." Attend local real estate investing club meetings and make friends with other investors. Throw parties for your investors, trades people and tenants. Head to Home Depot and shop until your heart is content because this

is for your investment! Male or female – real estate offers something for just about every kind of personality, which means you can create a business you love.

NOW MEN – HOW CAN YOU CONVINCE YOUR WIFE?

I've had the privilege of speaking to real estate investors all across Canada – from Victoria, British Columbia all the way to Halifax, Nova Scotia. When I step off stage I almost always get some version of this comment from at least one man in the audience:

"Oh, I really wish my wife had been here to listen to your talk. I want her to get into this with me but she's so worried. If she could hear someone like you talking about it, I think she would be interested!" or "I'd love my wife to be as into it as you are. How can I convince her?"

The number one rule of persuasion: You will never convince anybody to do anything. Period.

If you are trying to convince someone, they are going to dig their feet in further and hold on even tighter to what they think or believe. The only thing you can do is lead by example, and if someone shows interest, you can make an invitation.

ARE YOU SURE YOU WANT TO INVEST IN REAL ESTATE TOGETHER?

Investing together as a couple has tremendous rewards – but sometimes the challenges can feel insurmountable.

When we first began investing together in 2001, we had been dating for about 18 months. We treated all of our early investments like a joint venture. Each deal was a different transaction with a different agreement that we signed. Not every deal we did was together because we didn't always agree on what deals to do. We operated together when we agreed and separately when we didn't.

That worked for a year or so, and then things got rocky.

There was a lot going on in our relationship, and it was already under a lot of strain when one of our properties became a nightmare to manage. As part of a new purchase, we had inherited a blunt and demanding tenant. She was constantly fighting with the new basement-unit tenants, leaving me multiple voicemails every day, and finally escalating the situation to the point where the police were called twice in one week.

On top of that, a couple of Dave's investments turned out to be major lemons. Dave found himself in court defending fire code violations and dealing with a property manager charged with manslaughter.

It was too much for us to handle as a couple at the time, and we broke up for almost a full year. When we did get back together, we were drowning in debt, vacancies and renovations; and we were fighting to keep our head above water and fix our mistakes. It was a tough time for us as a couple and as real estate investors.

Maybe we would have had a bad patch in our relationship even if we hadn't been real estate investors. It was likely destined to be part of our journey anyway, but I can tell you with certainty that the fact that we were real estate investors together made *everything* way more difficult and stressful.

Even today it's our greatest challenge. It can be very difficult to make sound business decisions when you're emotionally involved with the person you're in business with. It can also be very difficult to turn off the "work talk" and just be husband and wife.

My husband Dave and I don't have the secret; we're still working at it. Real estate has given me a tremendous amount of financial security and freedom, and I am grateful for that. I love that my husband and I can take time off together whenever we want to and that together we create our schedule; but sometimes I just want a break. And it's hard to get that break when my business partner in both of my real estate related businesses is also my best friend and spouse.

I have a feeling every married couple that works together – regardless of what kind of business it is – has challenges; but here are seven of our biggest "lessons learned" and tips for gaining the support of your spouse and working together as investors.

Lack of spousal support holds a lot of people back. They try to convince their spouse to allow them to invest in real estate or to join them, but the fact is this:

You can't convince your spouse to do anything.

What you can do is create a shared *vision* of what you want your life to look like. With that vision firmly in place, you can then figure out how you can get there together.

Most people dream of a day when both parents can be there to pick up the kids from school or when you can take advantage of a last minute vacation deal without counting vacation days or asking permission from your boss. Few other investment opportunities out there can give you the kind of cash flow, wealth creation and freedom that real estate can give you. So if you start with creating a shared vision, you just might find you come to the same conclusion: it's time to invest in real estate!

Criticism is poisonous.

We all make mistakes. We all have bad days. But for some reason husbands and wives can say the meanest things to each other on those bad days. And when you invest together, there are going to be tough days!

When your spouse makes a mistake, they will feel bad enough. You won't have to say much at all; but if you must say something, keep it positive and not personal. For example, instead of saying something like: "What a stupid thing to have the painters come in after the carpet cleaners. Now we'll probably have to get the carpets cleaned a second time!" – you can say something like: "I think next time the carpet cleaners should come after the painters just in case the painters spill any paint on the carpet."

TIP 3: LEARN HOW TO LET OUT STEAM WITHOUT FIGHTING

You can find yourself getting into heated conversations without even realizing it. It happens to us all the time when we're frustrated over a bank decision, or a mistake made by a contractor or a difficult tenant. Instead of getting into a fight, we have little things we say to let the other person know it's getting heated without confronting them. For example, you could say to your spouse in a friendly tone "Okay, sergeant. Want me to do 20 push ups too?" or "Yes, Chicken Little, I know the sky is falling."

For us, usually just the simple gesture of placing a hand on the other person's arm can distill escalating emotions. It just makes us pause and think about what we're saying. Usually a pause is all you need; then you can take a breath and calm down to the point of having a constructive conversation instead of a fight.

TIP 4: MAKE EACH OTHER FEEL IMPORTANT

It's so easy to take people for granted, and for some reason it's even easier when you are married to each other. One of the easiest ways to keep your relationship strong as partners and as spouses is to appreciate each other and make each other feel important. One of the best things Dave said to me recently was that I was his "unfair advantage," I make it easier for him to find JV partners because of all the writing I do for publications like Canadian Real Estate Magazine. That made me feel important – and appreciated! I try to always let him know that he's important to me and to our business, and I know there is always room for more!!

I'm sure you've heard it said that "You don't know what you've got until it's gone." Don't let it get to that – recognize and acknowledge all you've got in your partner while it's here, and then it's more likely to stay!

When I walk into a property, I know within two minutes if it's one I want to own or not. There's still due diligence required to ensure it's a good deal, but, as mentioned, I won't buy anything I don't get a good feeling about.

That said, we could never sit across from a private lender, JV partner, or our mortgage broker, and say, "It's going to be a great deal because Julie says it 'feels good.'" That's where Dave comes in. He's got the details covered. He makes sure dozens of potential scenarios are accounted for and that we haven't missed a surprise expense or some other issue with the financial aspect of the home.

The early mistakes we made were either without joint consensus or during a moment when we both were in a highly emotional state. Today we're pretty consistent in the amount of money we make from our deals and that's because *we use our dramatically different approaches to our advantage.*

TIP 6: YOU WIN TOGETHER AND YOU LOSE TOGETHER

We coached a couple that had an under-performing property manager. We helped them let go of their property manager and take over management of their property themselves. The biggest issue we faced in helping them was their own issues as a couple. They didn't have established roles and responsibilities; and worse, it seemed like it was a contest regarding who was doing more work, and therefore, who should do *more*. We became mediators more than coaches because they were fighting about who should clean, who should show the house to tenants, and who was booking the carpet cleaning. The thing they weren't realizing is: *you lose together or you win together* – there is no in-between.

For us, we have general roles and responsibilities so we can operate smoothly. Dave is responsible for finding financing and joint venture partners. He is the primary contact for our property managers and tenants. He also generally works with our lawyer and accountant. I work on the marketing, and if renovation work needs to be done I coordinate it. Most other things (finding deals, structuring deals, negotiations) we do together.

These roles are not written in stone, though. I pitch in when Dave needs me and he pitches in when I need him. We are not competing against each other; we're going for a team win. Your perspective as an investing couple will change for the better if you take that approach.

TIP 7: DRAW THE LINE AND DON'T CROSS IT

Sometimes I don't even want to hear Dave talk. I know that sounds awful but when we don't turn off the real estate talk – even just for an hour or two a night – I get overwhelmed and exhausted. It's so easy to get excited about a deal or to want to troubleshoot a problem into the night, but the reality is that it isn't a healthy way to live. You'll wake up feeling tired, and instead of looking forward to being with each other as husband and wife, you'll feel like speaking to each other is just more work.

We are pretty extreme examples because we run *two* real estate businesses together – one investment business and one education-based business – so it can be all real estate all the time at our house. And we really enjoy what we do, so it's easy to spend a lot of time talking about it. However, we find we're happier together and more effective if we draw lines like:

- No real estate talk after 8pm;
- Phones off at meal times unless there's something important going on that has to be dealt with immediately;
- No real estate talk with friends unless they start and keep the conversation going on real estate;
- Designate real-estate-free days.

Real estate investing is not always easy, and it can definitely add stress to a relationship when something goes wrong – and something *will* go wrong; that's just how it is. But it can also be highly rewarding. So whether you're a man or a woman currently investing in real estate, you might want to consider gaining the support of your spouse and finding a way to work together.

So ladies, whether you choose to go solo or to team up with your spouse to create a powerful team, go for it! Either way, I look forward to seeing you at a real estate investing event soon and maybe at some point we'll share a stage together, helping others to further their real estate investing career!

CHAPTER FIFTEEN

IS REAL ESTATE FOR YOU?

I was reading an online real estate forum, and someone had posted that 80% of real estate investors fail in the first 5 years. The post then went on to say that of the 20% that survive their first 5 years, 80% of them will fail in the next five years.

If you're doing the math on that claim, it means that 96% of investors will fail within 10 years.

There was a really lively discussion going on in the forum about preventing failure and why so many fail. When I read it, I immediately had two thoughts.

First, the stat was bogus. The guy who posted this on the forum made it up. His objective for posting it was to invite you to work with him in his coaching program with the idea that his systems and processes would help you be the 4% that succeed. So not only did he make it up; it was solely for his own benefit that he posted it.

Second, in all of the discussion, *nobody* defined what failure actually was.

What does failure actually mean?

Maybe failure means that you have two property managers rob rent money from you ... or perhaps it means you buy properties in a troublesome area, where the only guy who would manage your properties ends up being charged with man-slaughter and you're left pleading with the courts to allow your property manager out at night so he can handle tenant issues.

Of course, by now you know that if that were the case, I'm a royal failure.

Maybe it means you've filed for bankruptcy. If that's the case, does that mean Donald Trump is a failure?

Probably not.

Failure is simple to me. *You only fail when you quit.*

Everything else is learning.

Of course some learning is more painful than others – *and my goal in writing this book has been to help you avoid much of the pain that we inflict upon ourselves when we allow ourselves to believe the myths and lies that are out there in the real estate industry.*

It's the pain we cause when we allow ourselves to believe that it's possible for one guy to buy 350 properties in his first year as an investor. It's the stress we bring into our lives when we chase deals all over the country in search of no-money-down deals, cash flow and motivated sellers. It's the exhaustion we feel when we try to invest in a city because it's on someone's Top 10 list, even if that city is not a good fit for our life.

In this book, I have shared things that few other investors in the public eye would admit to. I make mistakes all the time and I have openly shared many of them with you.

Too many people speaking on stages, writing books and teaching programs make it sound like they have it all figured out. They gloss over the hard times they've had or the problems they had to figure out when they started. I was on a panel for the World Money Show where one of my fellow panelists actually said to the audience "Between my deals and my clients' deals, I've seen it all."

When public figures and presenters hide the crap they deal with in their business, it makes it too easy to believe the lies and myths that are so dominant in this industry. And as I've discussed, those myths and lies can lead you into deals you shouldn't do. They can also leave you feeling tired, frustrated and discouraged when things go wrong.

And things *will* go wrong. You *will* make mistakes. But you don't have to fear those mistakes. Thankfully, real estate is fairly forgiving and you can make money even on some big mistakes!

Despite all the dramatic stories I've shared with you in this book, we've actually only lost money on one property – the Niagara Falls crack house. We were so desperate to get it out of our lives that we kept discounting its price until finally someone took that nightmare off our hands.

All things considered, we've made good money in the last eleven years and I am confident our most profitable deals are still ahead of us.

In this book, I haven't spent much time talking about the money you can make in real estate because there's enough talk and hype out there about the money one can make. When I wrote this book, I made the assumption that you probably wouldn't be reading it if you didn't already think real estate could do something good for you financially. What *I* wanted to do was to offer a realistic perspective – without the hyperbole and the false promises. I want you to be able to get into real estate investing with a better sense of what it involves – the great stuff and the not so great stuff.

My hope is that if you become a real estate investor *knowing* that it takes work, and knowing that it typically takes years, you're much less likely to get screwed and much more likely to get on a path that slowly and steadily makes you wealthy and that allows you to be in control of your time, your finances and your life.

I started this book with a confession: there are days where I think a job at Starbucks sounds great. There are times when our business totally stresses me out.

Please do not misunderstand what I'm saying though: leaving my job to get into full time real estate investing was the best decision I ever made. And leaving my job was the single biggest leap of faith in myself that I have ever taken!

I am grateful for the life I live.

We have 100% control over our time. When Dave's parents sold their house, and his Dad wanted to clean the basement out on a Monday & Tuesday, Dave went over there and helped. When the snow is incredible at Whistler, we head up there and ski, even if it's a Wednesday.

When we were presented with the opportunity to go to Africa with Greg Habstritt and his company for the opening of a school they had sponsored in a village in Uganda, we looked at our business, pulled out the cash we needed, and booked off the time! That trip to Africa was a once in a lifetime experience – one we'll never forget!

I had a job, *none* of this was possible.

But here's the piece I want to point out yet again:

Real estate didn't make that leap from worker bee to entrepreneur possible – I did. We hadn't reached a magic number of properties that ensured we were secure. Nor did we have anywhere near the cash coming in monthly to make it easy for me to say "no thanks" to my six-figure salary.

In this book, I've laid out the critical pieces of buy-and-hold real estate investing. My hope is that after reading it, you will have a greater sense of how to find good deals, create a unique advantage by being an area expert, fund those deals, and make money from them by finding great tenants.

Hopefully I've killed some of the big myths around real estate that get so many people into messes. I really hope that you'll question the information you consume – and not just trust it because you love someone's television show or because there's a famous name behind the course that's being offered.

The big real estate truths I want you to take away from this book are:

It takes a lot of perseverance; you're not doing something wrong if it seems difficult to find good deals. You just have to keep working at becoming an area expert and getting the word out about what kind of deals you're looking for.

It's not immediate – even the strategies that sound quick and lucrative, like wholesaling and sandwich leases, are an enormous amount of work and they take money, energy and effort to consistently make money doing them. There really isn't quick cash in real estate until you've invested a lot of time, money and energy to set up your business. Even then it's still not that quick.

There are a lot of famous people in the real estate business who are not telling you the truth. Some have licensed their name out and have nothing to do with the training, while others are only telling you part of the story. Just because someone is famous does not make them credible. Ask good questions. Many things are possible in real estate, but are they probable?

Real estate is likely the best long-term wealth creator, and over time it can offer you enormous financial and time freedom; but if you want to leave your job before you've got a bunch of properties paid off or an enormous portfolio, you're going to need something more than real estate to rely on for your cash today needs.

Nothing will happen if you don't take action!

Remember: even with the right systems, the right team, the right strategies for making more income every month, and a focused plan – it's not easy. You may meet real estate investors who pretend it's absolutely as easy as can be, but it's not.

IS REAL ESTATE THE ANSWER FOR YOU?

There is a romantic notion about the freedom you can create for yourself and your family as a real estate investor, but active real estate investing takes a *lot* of energy, effort and money! Even if you do it carefully and strategically, you are still creating a job for yourself – so you have to consider if it's a job you really want to do *for the long term.*

We've bought so many properties in the last three years that

I've lost track of how many we own, what the addresses are, and who the tenants are. It gets tiring always doing transactions, placing new tenants, and thinking through the strategy for every deal. There is a lot of effort that goes into being an area expert, generating a deal funnel, and raising the money needed for everything.

Nevertheless, you may find that it works for you as it has for us. OR you may find that real estate investing is the perfect wealth and retirement strategy for you AND that there is a business you can create or a job you love that will pay your bills every month.

OR real estate might not be the answer you're looking for. Again, I'm an enormous fan of real estate investing, but it's not the answer for everyone.

Real estate investing *is the perfect opportunity for some people.* If that is YOU, I know one thing for certain – there is only one thing holding you back from creating the life you love, and that is YOU.

Most people want to wait until the perfect moment to take a leap – whether the big move is into real estate or some other venture. The problem is that there is *never* a perfect time.

Marketer and entrepreneur Alex Mandossian says: "Sloppy success is better than perfect mediocrity." I agree ... and you don't *start* with perfection.

Philip McKernan (www.philipmckernan.com) argues that the pursuit of perfection pretty much guarantees unhappiness because perfection is impossible.

The situation where you can leave your job and start doing what you want to do – whether it's real estate investing or something else – is never going to be perfect. At some point you have to open the door to the dark stairway and take a step. You might trip, but chances are you'll put your foot out and find the first step and then the next. You just have to believe that either way you're going to be okay. If you *know* you want to do it, and you're not doing it, the only thing holding you back is YOU!

My saying is: "*The missing piece is always action.*"

If you're stuck, it's amazing what shows up when you just start moving forward.

Start with your WHY. Design what you want your typical day to look like, and then make every investing decision with that in mind. Take action, surround yourself with great support, and change your goals as you grow and evolve. You're not going to fail if you keep going; you only fail when you quit.

Most importantly – enjoy the ride.

RECOMMENDED RESOURCES MENTIONED IN THE BOOK

Keith Cunningham
Company: Keys to the Vault
Website: http://www.keystothevault.com/
Facebook: https://www.facebook.com/pages/Keith-J-Cunningham/113394059728
Twitter: https://twitter.com/keystothevault

Greg Head (Author) The Canadian Investors Guide to Secrets of the Real Estate Cycle
Website: http://thestrategicinvestor.wordpress.com/
Facebook: https://www.facebook.com/greg.head.58
Twitter: https://twitter.com/StrategicInvstr

Ian Kennedy
Company: Aspire REI
Website: http://www.aspirerealestate.ca/
Facebook: https://www.facebook.com/IanJKennedy
Twitter: https://twitter.com/AspireREI

Philip McKernan
Website: http://philipmckernan.com/
Facebook: https://www.facebook.com/PhilipMcKernanInc
Twitter: https://twitter.com/PhilipMcKernan

Michelle Pink
Company: Think Pink Real Estate Solution
Website: http://thinkpinkrealestate.ca/

Christine Ruptash (Author) The Canadian Investors Guide to Secrets of the Real Estate Cycle
Website: http://thestrategicinvestor.wordpress.com/
Facebook: https://www.facebook.com/christine.ruptash
Twitter: https://twitter.com/StrategicInvstr

Ian Szabo
Company: From Renos to Riches
Website: http://flipschool.ca/
Facebook: https://www.facebook.com/FlipSchoolCanada

Bill Walston
Company: Bill On Business
Website: http://www.billonbusiness.net/
Facebook: https://www.facebook.com/FlipSchoolCanada
Twitter: https://twitter.com/resherpa

WEBSITES

Canada Mortgage and Housing Corporation
Website: http://www.cmhc-schl.gc.ca/
Twitter: https://twitter.com/CMHC_ca

Statistics Canada
Website: http://www.statcan.gc.ca/start-debut-eng.html
Facebook: https://www.facebook.com/StatisticsCanada
Twitter: https://twitter.com/statcan_eng

United States Census Bureau
Website: http://www.census.gov/people/
Facebook: https://www.facebook.com/uscensusbureau
Twitter: https://twitter.com/uscensusbureau

RentoMeter
Website: http://www.rentometer.com/

Craigslist
Website: http://www.craigslist.org
Facebook: http://www.facebook.com/pages/craig-slist/101056018477
Twitter: https://twitter.com/craigslist

Kijiji
Website: http://www.kijiji.ca/
Facebook: https://www.facebook.com/Kijiji.ca
Twitter: https://twitter.com/Kijiji

Let's Talk Property Management
Website: http://www.letstalkpm.com/
Facebook: https://www.facebook.com/Kijiji.ca
Twitter: https://twitter.com/LetsTalkPM

Bigger Pockets
Website: http://www.biggerpockets.com/
Facebook: https://www.facebook.com/Kijiji.ca
Twitter: https://twitter.com/LetsTalkPM

E-Voice
Website: http://www.evoice.com/
Twitter: https://twitter.com/evoice

Meet Up
Website: http://www.meetup.com/
Facebook: https://www.facebook.com/Meetup
Twitter: https://twitter.com/Meetup

Docstoc
Website: http://www.docstoc.com/
Facebook: http://apps.facebook.com/docstoc_com/
Twitter: https://twitter.com/docstoc

Office of Housing and Constructing Standards
Website: http://www.rto.gov.bc.ca/

HotPads
Website: http://hotpads.com/

PadMapper
Website: http://www.padmapper.com
Facebook: https://www.facebook.com/pages/PadMapper/112488440458
Twitter: https://twitter.com/padmapper

Rental Homes Plus
Website: http://www.rentalhomesplus.com
Facebook: https://www.facebook.com/Rentalhomesplus
Twitter: https://twitter.com/RentalHomesPlus

Trulia
Website: http://www.trulia.com
Facebook: https://www.facebook.com/trulia
Twitter: https://twitter.com/trulia

Rental Properties.ca
Website: http://www.rentalproperties.ca

Rev N You YouTube Channel
Website: http://youtube.com/revnyou

RentSpot
Website: http://www.rentspot.com
Facebook: https://www.facebook.com/rentspot
Twitter: https://twitter.com/rentspot

View It.ca
Website: http://viewit.ca

Apartments.com
Website: http://www.apartments.com
Facebook: https://www.facebook.com/Apartments.com
Twitter: https://twitter.com/aptscom

Rent.com
Website: http://www.rent.com
Facebook: https://www.facebook.com/rentdotcom
Twitter: https://twitter.com/RentDotCom

Vista Print
Website: http://www.vistaprint.ca
Facebook: https://www.facebook.com/vistaprint
Twitter: https://twitter.com/Vistaprint

Rental Owners and Managers Association of British Columbia
Website: http://www.suites-bc.com/is now http://www.romsbc.com/
Facebook: https://www.facebook.com/romsbc
Twitter: https://twitter.com/ROMS_BC

DropBox
Website: https://www.dropbox.com/
Facebook: https://www.facebook.com/Dropbox
Twitter: https://twitter.com/Dropbox

Twitter
Website: https://twitter.com/
Facebook: https://www.facebook.com/Dropbox
Twitter: https://twitter.com/twitter

Facebook
Website: https://www.facebook.com/

Money Sense (Link to an article)
Website: http://www.moneysense.ca/2012/03/20/
top-35-best-places-to-live-in-2012/05_regina/)
Facebook: https://www.facebook.com/MoneySenseMagazine
Twitter: https://twitter.com/MoneySenseMag

Canadian Broadcasting Corporation – (link to a story on Rich Dad Poor Dad)
Website: http://www.cbc.ca/news/story/2010/01/28/consumer-rich-dad-poor-dad-marketplace.html

RECOMMENDED READING

The Canadian Investors Guide to Secrets of the Real Estate Cycle by Greg Head, Christine Ruptash, Keiran Trass and Don R. Campbell
The Psychology of Influence by Robert B. Cialdini
Pitch Anything by Oren Klaff
The Science of Influence by Kevin Hogan
The Psychology of Persuasion by Kevin Hogan
Canadian Real Estate Real Wealth Magazine

ABOUT THE AUTHOR

J ulie Broad was crazy enough to leave her six figure salary behind to become a full time investor at the age of 31. Today, after twelve years of owning properties in six different cities across Canada, overcoming a property manager charged with manslaughter, handling many bad tenants and raising millions of dollars in capital from investors, she knows exactly what it takes to succeed in real estate – and it's not what most tv personalities and authors will tell you. After leaving a career as a Vice President for Canada's leading real estate information services company, RealNet Canada, Julie became a sought after keynote speaker taking the stage across Canada for major events like the World Money Show and the Investor Forum series. She's also written hundreds of articles which have been published in Canadian Real Estate Wealth Magazine, the Vancouver Sun, Early to Rise and dozens of other North American online and offline newsletters, blogs and publications.

CPSIA information can be obtained at www.ICGtesting.com
Printed in the USA
LVOW13s2213020214

371985LV00003B/1093/P